MW00637996

SUPERSIZE
CROCHET ANIMALS

SUPERSIZE CROCHET ANIMALS

20 Adorable Amigurumi Sized to Snuggle

KRISTI SIMPSON

STACKPOLE BOOKS

Essex, Connecticut
Blue Ridge Summit, Pennsylvania

STACKPOLE BOOKS

Published by Stackpole Books
An imprint of Globe Pequot, the trade division of
The Rowman & Littlefield Publishing Group, Inc.
4501 Forbes Blvd., Ste. 200
Lanham, MD 20706
www.rowman.com

Distributed by NATIONAL BOOK NETWORK
800-462-6420

Copyright © 2022 Kristi Simpson
Photography by Heather Alvarado/Heartstrings Photography

All rights reserved. No part of this book may be reproduced in any form or by any electronic or mechanical means, including information storage and retrieval systems, without written permission from the publisher, except by a reviewer who may quote passages in a review.

The contents of this book are for personal use only. Patterns herein may be reproduced in limited quantities for such use. Any large-scale commercial reproduction is prohibited without the written consent of the publisher.

We have made every effort to ensure the accuracy and completeness of these instructions. We cannot, however, be responsible for human error, typographical mistakes, or variations in individual work.

British Library Cataloguing in Publication Information available

Library of Congress Cataloging-in-Publication Data is Available

ISBN 978-0-8117-7100-9 (paper: alk. paper)
ISBN 978-0-8117-7102-3 (electronic)

♾️™ The paper used in this publication meets the minimum requirements of American National Standard for Information Sciences—Permanence of Paper for Printed Library Materials, ANSI/NISO Z39.48-1992.

First Edition

CONTENTS

PATTERNS

Dax the Whale   6

Olivia the Owl   12

Flora Flamingo   18

Pinchy the Crab   24

Happy the Platypus   30

Chubb-Bee   36

Shelby the Sheep   42

Denton the Woolly Mammoth   48

INTRODUCTION

Amigurumi are cute crocheted stuffed animals or toys for young children. Typically, they are tiny creations, but I have taken the crocheted animal to a new supersize level and designed 20 huge animals for you to crochet just by using super bulky yarn! Seriously, the smallest is 14½ inches tall, and some are up to 19 inches tall! The collection has a creative variety ranging from Larry the Llama to Pinchy the Crab, with lots of options in between! Feel free to flip through and see how adorable some of these animals are . . . and how much the kiddos love 'em!

Crochet amigurumi is not difficult, and it can often be learned within a few days. And when you give a child one of these supersize (kid-size) amigurumi animals, they'll be asking for one of each before you know it!

When you look at an amigurumi piece, it can seem intimidating, but it's actually much easier than you might think. For beginners, it is easy and convenient to follow a pattern, especially with this book! I have prepared a "How to Read the Patterns" section and a full "Stitch Guide" with photo tutorials to help guide you through all the stitches and techniques used in this book. If you're a beginner, I would recommend starting with the Sweetheart

Hippo, as it uses only the basic stitches and keeps it simple. You will become familiar with the basic stitches, how to hold your hook, where to insert your hook, how to complete different stitches, and so on.

One of my favorite things about this book is that since we are using super bulky #6 yarn, the hook is not tiny. You'll be using a J (6 mm) or K (6.5 mm) hook most of the time. With a larger hook and yarn, you will be able to pull the yarn tighter more easily and see your work well as you complete your stitches. The yarn is easy to work with, and you'll love seeing the project come together quickly!

If you're a more advanced crocheter, you now have 20 new supersize amigurumi crochet patterns in your hands! Try Floppy the Frog, Flutter the Butterfly, Dax the Whale, Tucky the Turtle, Alton the Tiger . . . all of them! Who knows, you might learn something new!

Many crocheters love making cute, stuffed crocheted animals and toys for babies and young children, but these special gifts should be made as safe as possible, especially for children under the age of three. *Never attach anything to a toddler's or baby's toy or doll that can be pulled or chewed off and swallowed.* I have used safety eyes on most of

the animals, but a simple crocheted round eye, or circle, can be used instead.

As a general rule, the best yarn for amigurumi is medium-weight #4 yarn. However, this book is for supersize amigurumi. I created this collection with bulky #5 yarn, super bulky #6 yarn, or jumbo #7 yarn. By doing so, your animal will naturally be larger. If you use a medium-weight yarn instead of the super bulky yarn, you will have a "mini" version of the supersize animals. I had a few made up to show you the difference. If you want to make a mini version of your preferred animal, please keep in mind they are still going to be about 8 to 10 inches tall, not a typical small amigurumi! I would recommend using an F (3.75 mm) crochet hook and medium-weight yarn to make the mini version. Please be advised that the jumbo #7 yarn projects (Llama, Sheep, and Sloth) will not convert to a mini size due to the construction of the textured yarn.

When using super bulky #6 yarn, keep in mind that not all yarn is created equal. Some may be thicker, thinner, and/or spun differently. For instance, Bernat Baby Blanket (used in the Frog) is thicker than Berroco Coco (used in the Turtle and Dino). The Knit Picks (WeCrochet) Tuff Puff is like roving and not spun at all, so the texture is different. Even so, you do not have to have the exact gauge to create each of the animals. The finished size might be different, but the completed project will look great if you use consistent stitching throughout. Gauge is not as important with crochet amigurumi as it is with fit-to-size items like sweaters, slippers, hats, etc.

So, let's get busy! Find your yarn and have fun making this SUPERSIZE collection!

Best stitches,
Kristi

TIPS FOR CROCHET AMIGURUMI ANIMALS

When you crochet your animals, consider the following tips:

- When decreasing, use the invisible single crochet 2 together (sc2tog). Instructions are in each pattern's "Special Stitches" section when sc2tog is used. You'll love how smooth it looks compared to the traditional sc2tog.

- If you have gaps in your stitches, try using a smaller size hook, using a tighter tension, removing some stuffing, and/or using the invisible single crochet 2 together decrease. Using one or a few of these tips will help you have less gaps in your work.

- Most of the animals in this book are designed to have one body and head form. The key to keeping the head from being floppy around the neckline is STUFFING! Add stuffing, then add some more! Buy stuffing materials like Poly-fil stuffing in your local craft shop or online. Alternatively, a budget-friendly option is the filling from old cushions or pillows.

- Even when adding stuffing to the arms, legs, body, or other pieces, put as much stuffing as you can into the piece all at once in one big clump, then add more to the center of the clump if needed. The key is to only add stuffing in the middle, so the outside remains smooth and less lumpy. Put the stuffing in layer by layer, one on top of the other, until the piece is filled.

- Learn how to make the magic ring (sometimes called the magic circle). It allows you to pull the beginning round tightly so there isn't a hole in your work. I have also added it to the Stitch Guide (page 135) so you can see step by step how to complete this technique.

- Before adding the eyes, or any body part, stuff the body or head so you can see its shape. You can always remove the stuffing and continue your project, but it'll make the assembly easier as you complete the project.

- When joining the final round, use the invisible join. It allows the last join not to be just a slip stitch and knot, but makes the final stitch look like all the other stitches. It's easy, and directions can be found in your Stitch Guide (page 134).

- Count your stitches. In most of the patterns, rows and rounds vary in counts, so keep track! *Count!* It will save you time, I promise!

- Use stitch markers. Keep a stash to use to mark where the eyes will go or where you want to add the arms and legs. They can be used in many different ways beyond just marking your starting stitch.

- When sewing on your pieces, use a yarn needle or two to hold the item in place. Use them like pins to secure the pieces, or you can also use stitch markers.

PATTERNS

Dax the Whale

This giant amigurumi whale is the ultimate stuffed animal! Your kids will love playing with him, and he is likely to become their new best friend. His playful stitch will keep you swimming back for more crochet time!

Yarn

Cascade Yarns Pacific Bulky; super bulky weight #6; 60% acrylic/40% superwash merino wool; 7.05 oz (200 g)/129 yds (118 m) per skein
- 3 skeins: 159 Dusty Turquoise (**A**)
- 1 skein each: 116 Lamb (**B**), 01 White (**C**)

Hook and Other Materials

- US size J-10 (6 mm) crochet hook
- Yarn needle
- Two 15 mm safety eyes
- Poly-fil stuffing
- Stitch markers

Finished Measurement

About 22 in (56 cm) long

Gauge

11 sc and 11 rows/rounds = 4 in (10 cm)
Adjust hook size if necessary to obtain gauge.

Special Stitch

Invisible single crochet 2 together (sc2tog): Insert hook in the FLO of next 2 sts, yarn over and draw through both sts, yarn over and draw through 2 loops on hook (1 stitch decreased).

Pattern Note

Dax the Whale is made in 7 pieces: Body, 2 Tail Fins, 2 Side Fins, Spout, and Belly.

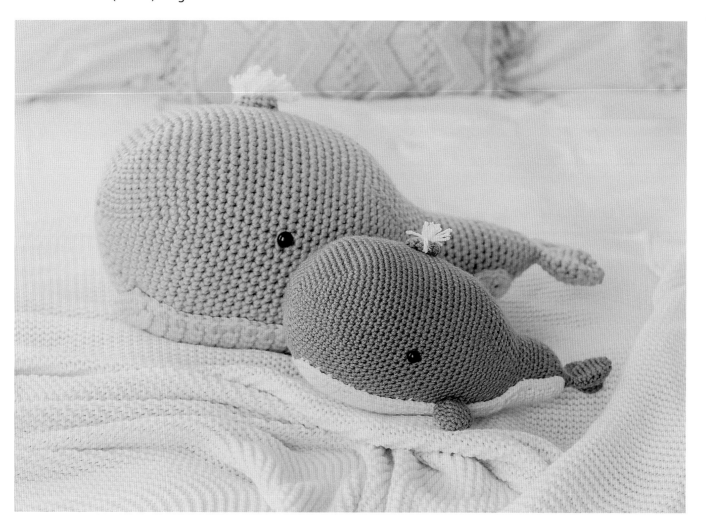

INSTRUCTIONS

Body

Rnd 1 (RS): With **A**, create magic ring, 6 sc in ring; do not join. (6 sc) Place marker to indicate beginning of rnd.

Note: Loop a short piece of yarn around any stitch to mark Rnd 1 as right side. Move stitch marker up with each rnd.

Rnd 2: 2 sc in each st around. (12 sc)

Rnd 3: (Sc in next st, 2 sc in next st) around. (18 sc)

Rnd 4: (Sc in next 2 sts, 2 sc in next st) around. (24 sc)

Rnd 5: (Sc in next 3 sts, 2 sc in next st) around. (30 sc)

Rnd 6: (Sc in next 4 sts, 2 sc in next st) around. (36 sc)

Rnd 7: (Sc in next 5 sts, 2 sc in next st) around. (42 sc)

Rnd 8: (Sc in next 6 sts, 2 sc in next st) around. (48 sc)

Rnd 9: (Sc in next 7 sts, 2 sc in next st) around. (54 sc)

Rnd 10: (Sc in next 8 sts, 2 sc in next st) around. (60 sc)

Rnd 11: (Sc in next 9 sts, 2 sc in next st) around. (66 sc)

Rnd 12: (Sc in next 10 sts, 2 sc in next st) around. (72 sc)

Rnds 13–35: Sc in each st around.

Rnd 36: (Sc in next 10 sts, sc2tog) 4 times, sc in each st around. (68 sc)

Rnd 37: (Sc in next 9 sts, sc2tog) 4 times, sc in each st around. (64 sc)

Rnd 38: (Sc in next 8 sts, sc2tog) 4 times, sc in each st around. (60 sc)

Rnd 39: (Sc in next 7 sts, sc2tog) 4 times, sc in each st around. (56 sc)

Rnd 40: (Sc in next 6 sts, sc2tog) 4 times, sc in each st around. (52 sc)

Rnd 41: (Sc in next 5 sts, sc2tog) 4 times, sc in each st around. (48 sc)

Rnd 42: (Sc in next 6 sts, sc2tog) around. (42 sc)

Rnd 43: Sc in each st around.

Rnd 44: (Sc in next 5 sts, sc2tog) around. (36 sc)
Stuff Body firmly.

Lay Body with the decreased section on top. Add safety eyes between Rnds 25 and 26 on each side about 39 sts apart.

Rnds 45–46: Sc in each st around.

Rnd 47: (Sc in next 4 sts, sc2tog) around. (30 sc)

Rnds 48–49: Sc in each st around.

Rnd 50: Sc2tog, sc in each st around. (29 sc)

Rnd 51: Sc in each st around.

Rnd 52: Sc2tog, sc in each st around. (28 sc)

Rnd 53: Sc in each st around.

Rnd 54: Sc2tog, sc in each st around. (27 sc)

Rnd 55: (Sc in next 7 sts, sc2tog) around. (24 sc)

Rnd 56: (Sc in next 6 sts, sc2tog) around. (21 sc)
Stuff firmly.

Rnd 57: Sc in each st around.

Rnd 58: (Sc in next 5 sts, sc2tog) around. (18 sc)

Rnd 59: (Sc in next 4 sts, sc2tog) around. (15 sc)

Rnd 60: Sc in each st around.

Rnd 61: (Sc in next 3 sts, sc2tog) around. (12 sc)
Do not fasten off.
Stuff firmly.

Tail Fin 1

Rnd 1: Sc in next 5 sts, sk 6 sts, sc in next st; do not join. (6 sc)

Rnd 2: (Sc in next st, 2 sc in next st) around. (9 sc)

Rnd 3: (Sc in next 2 sts, 2 sc in next st) around. (12 sc)

Rnd 4: Sc in each st around.

Rnd 5: (Sc in next 3 sts, 2 sc in next st) around. (16 sc)

Rnd 6: Sc in each st around.

Rnd 7: (Sc in next 3 sts, sc2tog) around. (12 sc)

Rnd 8: (Sc in next 2 sts, sc2tog) around. (9 sc)

Rnd 9: (Sc in next st, sc2tog) around. (6 sc)

Fasten off, leaving a long tail for closing.

Thread yarn needle and close Rnd 9.

Tail Fin 2

Pull up a loop of **A** in next unworked st of Rnd 61 of Body, ch 1, sc in next 6 sts; do not join. (6 sc)

Rnds 2–9: Repeat Rnds 2–9 of Fin 1.

Side Fins (make 2)

Rnd 1 (RS): With **A**, create magic ring, 4 sc in ring; do not join. (4 sc) Place marker to indicate beginning of rnd.

Note: Loop a short piece of yarn around any stitch to mark Rnd 1 as right side. Move stitch marker up with each rnd.

Rnd 2: 2 sc in each st around. (8 sc)

Rnd 3: Sc in each st around.

Rnd 4: (Sc in next st, 2 sc in next st) around. (12 sc)

Rnd 5: (Sc in next 2 sts, 2 sc in next st) around. (16 sc)

Rnd 6: Sc in each st around.

Rnd 7: (Sc in next 2 sts, sc2tog) around. (12 sc)

Rnd 8: (Sc in next st, sc2tog) around. (8 sc)

Rnd 9: Sc in each st around; join with sl st to first sc.

Fasten off, leaving a long tail for sewing.

Do not stuff.

Belly

With **B**, ch 12.

Row 1 (RS): Sc in 2nd ch from hook and in each ch across, turn. (11 sc)

Rows 2–4: Ch 1, sc in each st across, turn.

Row 5: Ch 1, 2 sc in first st, sc in next 9 sts, 2 sc in next st, turn. (13 sc)

Rows 6–7: Ch 1, sc in each st across, turn.

Row 8: Ch 1, 2 sc in first st, sc in next 11 sts, 2 sc in next st, turn. (15 sc)

Rows 9–13: Ch 1, sc in each st across, turn.

Row 14: Ch 1, 2 sc in first st, sc in next 13 sts, 2 sc in next st, turn. (17 sc)

Rows 15–17: Ch 1, sc in each st across, turn.

Row 18: Ch 1, 2 sc in first st, sc in next 15 sts, 2 sc in next st, turn. (19 sc)

Rows 19–38: Ch 1, sc in each st across, turn.

Row 39: Ch 1, sc2tog, sc in next 15 sts, sc2tog, turn. (17 sc)

Rows 40–42: Ch 1, sc in each st across, turn.

Row 43: Ch 1, sc2tog, sc in next 13 sts, sc2tog, turn. (15 sc)

Rows 44–46: Ch 1, sc in each st across, turn.

Row 47: Ch 1, sc2tog, sc in next 11 sts, sc2tog, turn. (13 sc)

Row 48: Ch 1, sc in each st across, turn.

Row 49: Ch 1, sc2tog, sc in next 9 sts, sc2tog, turn. (11 sc)

Row 50: Ch 1, sc2tog, sc in next 7 sts, sc2tog, turn. (9 sc)

Row 51: Ch 1, sc2tog, sc in next 5 sts, sc2tog, do not turn. (7 sc)

Belly Trim

Rnd 1: Ch 1, sc 50 evenly down ends of rows, sc 11 across Row 1, sc 50 evenly down ends of rows, sc2tog, sc in next 3 sts, sc2tog; join with sl st to first sc. (116 sc)

Fasten off, leaving a long tail for sewing.

Spout

With **A**, ch 4.

Rnd 1 (RS): 9 dc in 4th ch from hook; join with sl st to beg ch-4. (10 dc)

Rnd 2: Ch 1, working in the BLO, sc in each st around; join with sl st to first sc.

Fasten off, leaving a long tail for sewing.

Cut ten 3 in (7.6 cm) strands of **C**. Fold strand in half, pull center around dc post, pull ends through center loop and pull tight. Repeat with all strands and trim evenly.

Use yarn needle to sew the Spout on top center of Body using the exposed loops from Rnd 2.

Assembly

Use photos as a guide.

Sew Belly to base of Body between Rnds 10 and 56.

Sew Side Fins to Body.

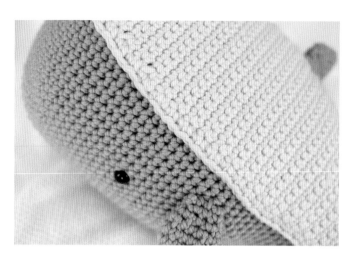

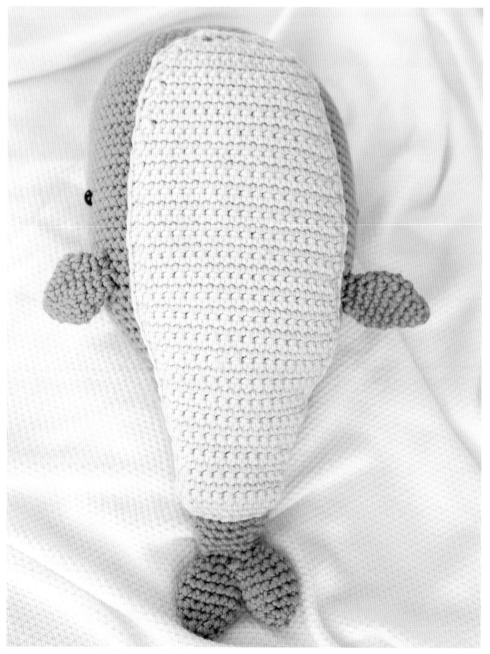

Olivia the Owl

The cuteness of this owl is so heartwarming! I made this as a mini for my niece when she was a baby, but as she's growing up, I've upsized her owl! It's adorable to see how much my niece truly loves this giant amigurumi. The stitching in the feathers shines and makes this an enviable baby shower gift, in giant or mini version.

Yarn

Premier Yarns Parfait Chunky; super bulky #6; 100% superwash merino; 3.5 oz (100 g)/131 yd (120 m) per skein
- 6 skeins: 1150-06 Mint (**A**)
- 1 skein: 1150-12 Sunshine (**B**) (nose only)

Premier Yarns Anti-Pilling Everyday Bulky; super bulky #6; 100% anti-pilling acrylic; 3.5 oz (100 g)/87 yd (80 m) per skein
- 1 skein: 1068-19 Cream (**C**)

Hook and Other Materials

- US size J-10 (6 mm) crochet hook
- Yarn needle
- Poly-fil stuffing
- Two 15 mm safety eyes
- Stitch markers

Finished Measurement

About 18 in (45.5 cm) tall

Gauge

11 sc and 11 rows/rounds = 4 in (10 cm)
Adjust hook size if necessary to obtain gauge.

MINI: Yarn, Hook, and Other Materials

I Love This Yarn!; medium weight #4; 100% acrylic; 7 oz (199 g)/355 yd (325 m) per skein
- 1 skein each: 230 Light Peach (**A**), 10 White (**B**), 330 Yellow (**C**)

US size F (3.75 mm) crochet hook
Two 12 mm safety eyes
Gauge for mini: 16 sts and 18 rows/round = 4 in (10 cm)

Special Stitches

Invisible single crochet 2 together (sc2tog): Insert hook in the FLO of next 2 sts, yarn over and draw through both sts, yarn over and draw through 2 loops on hook (1 stitch decreased).

Crocodile stitch (CS): Starting at the top, 4 dc down the post, ch 1, starting at the bottom, 4 dc up the next post.

Pattern Note

Olivia Owl is made in 8 sections: Body, Head, 2 Eyes, 2 Ears, and 2 Wings.

INSTRUCTIONS

Body

Rnd 1 (RS): With **A**, create magic ring, 8 sc in ring; do not join. (8 sc). Place marker to indicate beginning of rnd.

Note: Loop a short piece of yarn around any stitch to mark Rnd 1 as right side. Move stitch marker up with each rnd.

Rnd 2: 2 sc in each st around. (16 sc)

Rnd 3: (Sc in next st, 2 sc in next st) around. (24 sc)

Rnd 4: (Sc in next 2 sts, 2 sc in next st) around. (32 sc)

Rnd 5: (Sc in next 3 sts, 2 sc in next st) around. (40 sc)

Rnd 6: (Sc in next 4 sts, 2 sc in next st) around. (48 sc)

Rnd 7: (Sc in next 5 sts, 2 sc in next st) around. (56 sc)

Rnd 8: (Sc in next 6 sts, 2 sc in next st) around. (64 sc)

Rnd 9: (Sc in next 7 sts, 2 sc in next st) around. (72 sc)

Rnd 10: (Sc in next 8 sts, 2 sc in next st) around. (80 sc)

Rnd 11: (Sc in next 9 sts, 2 sc in next st) around. (88 sc)

Rnds 12–17: Sc in each st around.

Rnd 18: Sc in each st around; join with sl st to first sc.

Rnd 19: Ch 3 (counts as dc), dc in each st around; join with sl st to beg ch-3. (88 dc)

Rnd 20: Ch 3 (counts as first dc in CS), 3 dc down same post as joining, ch 1, starting at the bottom, 4 dc up next post to complete the first CS, sk 2 dc, *CS on next 2 sts, sk 2 dc; rep from * around; join with sl st to ch-3 of beg ch-3. (22 Crocodile stitches)

Rnd 21: Ch 3, dc over the ends of joined CS in middle of previous rnd skipped 2-dc, *2 dc in center of next CS, 2 dc in sp between previous rnd skipped 2-dc; rep from * around; join with sl st to beg ch-3. (88 dc)

Rnds 22–30: Repeat Rnds 20 and 21, ending on Rnd 20.

Rnd 31: Ch 1, 2 sc over the ends of joined CS in middle of previous rnd skipped 2-dc, *2 sc in center of next CS, 2 sc in sp between previous rnd skipped 2-dc; rep from * around; join with sl st to first sc. (88 sc)

Rnd 32: Ch 1, sc in each st around; do not join.

Rnds 33–34: Sc in each st around.

Rnd 35: (Sc in next 6 sts, sc2tog) around. (77 sc)

Rnd 36: (Sc in next 5 sts, sc2tog) around. (66 sc)

Rnd 37: (Sc in next 4 sts, sc2tog) around. (55 sc)

Rnd 38: (Sc in next 3 sts, sc2tog) around. (44 sc)

Stuff Body firmly.

Head

Rnd 39: (Sc in next 3 sts, 2 sc in next st). (55 sc)

Rnd 40: (Sc in next 4 sts, 2 sc in next st). (66 sc)

Rnd 41: (Sc in next 5 sts, 2 sc in next st). (77 sc)

Rnds 42–61: Sc in each st around.

Rnd 62: (Sc in next 5 sts, sc2tog) around. (66 sc)

Rnd 63: (Sc in next 4 sts, sc2tog) around. (55 sc)

Rnd 64: (Sc in next 3 sts, sc2tog) around. (44 sc)

Rnd 65: (Sc in next 2 sts, sc2tog) around. (33 sc)

Stuff Head firmly.

Rnd 66: (Sc in next st, sc2tog) around. (22 sc)

Rnd 67: (Sc2tog) 11 times. (11 sc)

Fasten off, leaving a long tail for sewing.

Use yarn needle with long tail and close Rnd 67.

Wing (make 2)

Rnd 1 (RS): With **A**, create magic ring, 8 sc in ring; do not join. (8 sc) Place marker to indicate beginning of rnd.

Note: Loop a short piece of yarn around any stitch to mark Rnd 1 as right side. Move stitch marker up with each rnd.

Rnd 2: 2 sc in each st around. (16 sc)

Rnd 3: (Sc in next st, 2 sc in next st) around. (24 sc)

Rnd 4: (Sc in next 2 sc, 2 sc in next st) around. (32 sc)

Rnds 5–11: Sc in each st around.

Rnd 12: (Sc in next 2 sts, sc2tog). (24 sc)

Rnd 13: (Sc in next st, sc2tog). (16 sc)

Fasten off, leaving a long tail for sewing to Body. Do not stuff.

Eye (make 2)

Rnd 1 (RS): With **C,** create magic ring, 6 sc in ring; do not join. (6 sc) Place marker to indicate beginning of rnd.

Note: Loop a short piece of yarn around any stitch to mark Rnd 1 as right side. Move stitch marker up with each rnd.

Rnd 2: 2 sc in each st around. (12 sc)

Rnd 3: (Sc in next st, 2 sc in next st) around. (18 sc)

Rnd 4: (Sc in next 2 sts, 2 sc in next st) around. (24 sc)

Rnd 5: (Sc in next 3 sts, 2 sc in next st) around. (30 sc)

Rnd 6: (Sc in next 4 sts, 2 sc in next st) around. (36 sc)

Fasten off, leaving a long tail for sewing to Head.

Ear (make 2)

Rnd 1 (RS): With **A**, create magic ring, 4 sc in ring; do not join. (4 sc) Place marker to indicate beginning of rnd.

Note: Loop a short piece of yarn around any stitch to mark Rnd 1 as right side. Move stitch marker up with each rnd.

Rnd 2: 2 sc in each st around. (8 sc)

Rnd 3: Sc in each st around.

Rnd 4: (Sc in next st, 2 sc in next st) around. (12 sc)

Rnd 5: Sc in each st around.

Rnd 6: (Sc in next 2 sts, 2 sc in next st) around. (16 sc)

Fasten off, leaving a long tail for sewing to Head. Do not stuff.

Assembly

Use photos as a guide.

Sew Wings to Body.

Sew Ears to Head.

Sew Eyes to Head.

Finishing

With **B,** stitch nose between Eyes with yarn needle.

Using **A,** cut 12 lengths of yarn 6 in (15.2 cm) long.

Fold in half, pull center loop of folded strip through closed Rnd 67 at top of Head, pull ends through the center loop. Repeat around and trim.

Flora Flamingo

This flamingo brings all the sass to the supersize amigurumi world! Her lanky legs help her strut her crochet stuff and stand tall above all the other animals! You'll love how easy she works up, and with the textured wings, she's super soft!

Yarn

Lion Brand Yarns Wool-Ease Thick & Quick; super bulky weight #6; 80% acrylic/20% wool; 6 oz (170 g)/106 yd (97 m) per skein
- 4 skeins: 640-102 Rouge (**A**)
- 1 skein each: 640-99 Fisherman (**B**), 640-153 Black (**C**)

Lion Brand Yarns Go For Faux Thick & Quick; jumbo weight #7; 100% polyester; 4.2 oz (120 g)/ 24 yd (22 m) per skein
- 3 skeins: 323-205 Pink Poodle (**D**)

Hooks and Other Materials
- US size J-10 (6 mm) crochet hook
- US size N-13 (9 mm) crochet hook
- Yarn needle
- Poly-fil stuffing
- Two 15 mm safety eyes
- Stitch markers

Finished Measurement

About 21 in (53 cm) tall

Gauge

With **A** and smaller hook, 11 sc and 11 rows/rounds = 4 in (10 cm).

Special Stitch

Invisible single crochet 2 together (sc2tog): Insert hook in the FLO of next 2 sts, yarn over and draw through both sts, yarn over and draw through 2 loops on hook (1 stitch decreased).

Pattern Notes
- Flamingo is made in 10 pieces: Body/Neck/Head, Beak, 2 Eyes, 2 Feet, 2 Legs, and 2 Wings.
- If creating a mini version, keep in mind the Wings are jumbo #7 yarn. I would recommend doubling your medium #4 yarn for the Wings OR crocheting the Wings according to pattern and wrapping the Wing edges in D for the extra detail and softness.

INSTRUCTIONS

Body

Beg at back end of Body, with smaller hook and **A**, ch 2.

Rnd 1: Work 6 sc in 2nd ch from hook; do not join, work in continuous rnds (spiral). Place a marker in last st made to indicate end of rnd. Move marker up as each rnd is completed.

Rnd 2: Sc in each st around.

Rnd 3: Work 2 sc in each st around. (12 sc)

Rnd 4: Sc in each st around.

Rnd 5: *Sc in next st, 2 sc in next st; rep from * around. (18 sc)

Rnd 6: Sc in each st around.

Rnd 7: Sc in each st around.

Rnd 8: *Sc in next 2 sts, 2 sc in next st; rep from * around. (24 sc)

Rnd 9: Sc in each st around.

Rnd 10: *Sc in next 3 sts, 2 sc in next st; rep from * around. (30 sc)

Rnd 11: *Sc in next 4 sts, 2 sc in next st; rep from * around. (36 sc)

Rnds 12–13: Sc in each st around.

Rnd 14: *Sc in next 5 sts, 2 sc in next st; rep from * around. (42 sc)

Rnd 15: Sc in each st around.

Rnd 16: *Sc in next 6 sts, 2 sc in next st; rep from * around. (48 sc)

Rnd 17: Sc in each st around.

Rnd 18: *Sc in next 7 sts, 2 sc in next st; rep from * around. (54 sc)

Rnd 19: Sc in each st around.

Rnd 20: *Sc in next 8 sts, 2 sc in next st; rep from * around. (60 sc)

Rnd 21: Sc in each st around.

Rnd 22: *Sc in next 9 sts, 2 sc in next st; rep from * around. (66 sc)

Rnds 23–24: Sc in each st around.

Rnd 25: *Sc in next 10 sts, 2 sc in next st; rep from * around. (72 sc)

Rnds 26–45: Sc in each st around.

Place a marker in Rnd 40 to indicate where sts will be sewn to shape bottom of Neck.

Rnd 46: *Sc in next 10 sts, sc2tog; rep from * around. (66 sc)

Rnd 47: *Sc in next 9 sts, sc2tog; rep from * around. (60 sc)

Rnd 48: *Sc in next 4 sts, sc2tog; rep from * around. (50 sc)

Rnd 49: *Sc in next 3 sts, sc2tog; rep from * around. (40 sc)

Rnd 50: *Sc in next 2 sts, sc2tog; rep from * around. (30 sc)

Stuff Body firmly.

Rnd 51: *Sc in next st, sc2tog; rep from * around. (20 sc)

Neck

Note: Stuff the Neck firmly as your work progresses.

Rnd 52: *Sc in next 2 sts, sc2tog; rep from * around. (15 sc)

Rnds 53–88: Sc in each st around.

Place a marker in Rnd 74 to indicate where sts will be sewn to shape bottom of Neck.

Place a marker in Rnd 80 to indicate where sts will be sewn to shape top of Neck.

Bend Neck up and sew marked Rnds 74 and 40 together with 3 sts to hold Neck in place to Body.

Remove the marker from Rnd 40.

Head

Rnd 89: *Sc in next 2 sts, 2 sc in next st; rep from * around. (20 sc)

Rnd 90: *Sc in next st, 2 sc in next st; rep from * around. (30 sc)

Rnd 91: *Sc in next 2 sts, 2 sc in next st; rep from * around. (40 sc)

Rnd 92: Sc in each st around.

Place a marker in Rnd 93 to indicate where sts will be sewn to Rnd 80.

Rnds 93–100: Sc in each st around.

Bend top of Neck down and sew marked Rnds 93 and 80 together with 3 sts to hold Head in place. Remove markers.

Rnd 101: *Sc in next 3 sts, sc2tog; rep from * around. (32 sc)

Rnd 102: Sc in each st around.

Rnd 103: *Sc in next 2 sts, sc2tog; rep from * around. (24 sc)

Rnd 104: Sc in each st around.

Rnd 105: *Sc in next st, sc2tog; rep from * around; join with sl st in first sc of this rnd. (16 sc) Remove end of rnd marker. Fasten off.

Following package directions, attach a safety eye to each side of Head between Rnds 102 and 103 about 10 sts apart.

Beak

Note: Read the Beak instructions carefully before beginning. Some rnds are worked as continuous rnds (spiral), but others are worked as joined rnds.

Rnd 106: Join **B** with sl st in a st of Rnd 105 that is on the underside of the Head, ch 1, sc in same st as joining sl st and in each sc around (take care not to work into the joining sl st of Rnd 105); join with sl st in first sc. (16 sc)

Rnd 107: Ch 1, sc in each st around; join with sl st to first sc.

Rnd 108: Ch 1, sc in each st around; join with sl st to first sc. Fasten off.

Rnd 109: Join **C** with sl st in a st of 108, ch 1, sc in each st around; join with sl st in first sc of this rnd.

Stuff Head and Beak firmly.

Rnd 110: Ch 1, *sc in next 2 sts, sc2tog; rep from * around; join with sl st in first sc. (12 sc)

Rnd 111: Ch 1, sc in each st around; join with sl st in first sc.

Rnd 112: Ch 1, (sc2tog) 6 times; join with sl st in first sc. (6 sc)

Rnd 113: Ch 1, sc in each st around; join with sl st in first sc.

Fasten off, leaving a long yarn tail for sewing. Stuff remainder of Beak lightly, leaving last 3 rnds unstuffed.

Thread yarn tail onto blunt needle and sew Rnds 113 and 111 together to pull Beak downward.

Wing (make 2)

With **D** and larger hook, ch 4.

Row 1: Work 2 dc in 4th ch from hook (3 skipped ch count as dc). (3 dc)

Row 2: Ch 3 (counts as dc), turn, dc in first st (increase made), dc in next st, 2 dc in top of beg ch-3. (5 dc)

Row 3: Ch 3 (counts as dc), turn, sk first st, dc in next st, 2 dc in next st, dc in next st, dc in top of beg ch-3. (6 dc)

Row 4: Ch 3 (counts as dc), turn, dc in first st, dc in next 4 sts, 2 dc in top of beg ch-3. (8 dc)

Row 5: Ch 3 (counts as dc), turn, dc in first st, dc in next 2 sts, 2 dc in next 2 sts, dc in next 2 sts, 2 dc in top of beg ch-3. (12 dc)

Row 6: Ch 3 (counts as dc), turn, dc in first st, dc in next 4 sts, 2 dc in next 2 sts, dc in next 4 sts, 2 dc in top of beg ch-3. (16 dc)

Rows 7–8: Ch 3 (counts as dc), turn, sk first dc, dc in each st across working last dc in top of beg ch-3.

Row 9: Ch 3 (counts as dc), turn, sk first 2 sts, dc in next 12 sts, sk next st, dc in top of beg ch-3. (14 dc)

Row 10: Ch 3 (counts as dc), turn, sk first 2 sts, dc in next 10 sts, sk next st, dc in top of beg ch-3. (12 dc)

Row 11: Ch 3 (counts as dc), turn, sk first 2 sts, dc in next 8 sts, sk next st, dc in top of beg ch-3. (10 dc)

Row 12: Ch 3 (counts as dc), turn, sk first 2 sts, dc in next 6 sts, sk next st, dc in top of beg ch-3. (8 dc)

Row 13: Turn, sc2tog, sc in next 4 sts, sc2tog (working over last dc and beg ch-3). (6 sc)

Row 14: Turn, sc2tog, sc in next 2 sts, sc2tog. (4 sc)

Leg (make 2)

Foot

Beg at end of Foot, with smaller hook and **B**, ch 21.

Rnd 1 (RS): Sc in 2nd ch from hook and in each ch across; join with sl st to first sc. (20 sc)

Rnd 2: Ch 1, sc in next 4 sts, sc2tog, sc in next 8 sts, sc2tog, sc in next 4 sts; do not join. (18 sc)

Rnd 3: Sc in next 4 sts, sc2tog, sc in next 6 sts, sc2tog, sc in next 4 sts. (16 sc)

Rnd 4: Sc in next 3 sts, sc2tog, sc in next 6 sts, sc2tog, sc in next 3 sts. (14 sc)

Rnd 5: Sc in next 3 sts, sc2tog, sc in next 4 sts, sc2tog, sc in next 3 sts. (12 sc)

Rnd 6: Sc in each st around. (12 sc)

Rnd 7: Sc in next 2 sts, sc2tog, sc in next 4 sts, sc2tog, sc in next 2 sts. (10 sc)

Heel

Rows 1–2: Ch 1, sc in next 5 sts, turn. (5 sc).

Row 3 (RS): Ch 1, sc2tog, sc in next st, sc2tog, turn. (3 sc)

Row 4 (WS): Ch 1, sc3tog, turn. (1 sc)

Place a marker in Row 4 st.

Leg

Rnd 1 (RS): Ch 1, working in the ends of rows, sc in next 4 sts; working across foot, sc2tog, sc in next st, sc2tog; working in ends of rows, sc in next 4 sts, sk marked st, sl st to next st, turn. (11 sts)

Remove stitch marker.

Rnd 2: Ch 1, sc2tog, sc in each st around; do not join; work in continuous rnds (spiral). (10 sts)

Place a marker in last st made to indicate end of rnd. Move marker up as each rnd is completed.

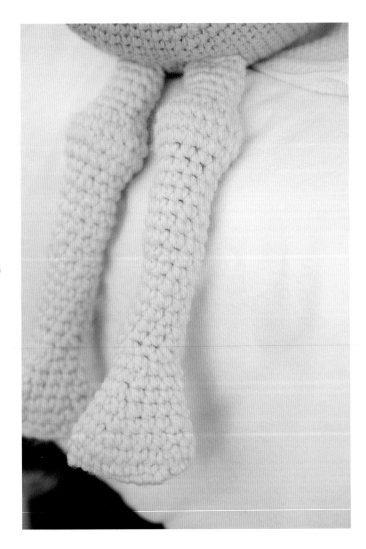

Rnds 7–14: Sc in each st around.
Rnd 15: 2 sc in each st around. (20 sc)
Rnds 16–17: Sc in each st around.
Rnd 18: (Sc2tog) 10 times. (10 sc)
Rnds 19–33: Sc in each st around.
Fasten off, leaving a long tail for sewing.

Assembly

Use photos as a guide.
Sew Legs to Body.
Sew Wings to Body, lining up last row of Wing with the Neck and overlapping the top edges of the Wings over the back of the flamingo.
Leave the lower edge of each Wing unsewn so it moves freely.

Pinchy the Crab

One of my favorite facts about crabs is that they can walk in all directions, but they mostly walk and run sideways. Can't you see those little legs moving at super speeds across the sand? Well, you don't have to worry about this crab scurrying away, because he's here to stay! Crochet him and his mini as friendly pillow pals for your little ones.

Yarn

Lion Brand Yarns Wool-Ease Thick & Quick; super bulky #6; 80% acrylic/20% wool; 6 oz (170 g)/106 yd (97 m) per skein
- 4 skeins: 640-137 Terracotta (**A**)
- 1 skein each: 640-153 Black (**B**), 640-99 Fisherman (**C**)

Hook and Other Materials
- US size J-10 (6 mm) crochet hook
- Yarn needle
- Poly-fil stuffing
- Stitch markers

Finished Measurement

Diameter (not including eyes): About 16½ in (42 cm)

Gauge

11 sc and 11 rows/rounds = 4 in (10 cm)

MINI: Yarn, Hook, and Other Materials

I Love This Yarn!; medium weight #4; 100% acrylic; 7 oz (199 g)/355 yd (325 m) per skein
- 1 skein each: 364 Glacier (**A**), 30 Black (**B**), 10 White (**C**)

US size F (3.75 mm) crochet hook

Gauge for mini: 16 sts and 18 rows/round = 4 in (10 cm)

Special Stitch

Invisible single crochet 2 together (sc2tog): Insert hook in the FLO of next 2 sts, yarn over and draw through both sts, yarn over and draw through 2 loops on hook (1 stitch decreased).

Pattern Notes
- Crab is made in 11 pieces: Body, 2 Eyes, 6 Feet, and 2 Pincers.
- Pieces are stuffed and then sewn together to make the crab.

INSTRUCTIONS

Body

Front

Rnd 1 (RS): With **A**, create magic ring, 8 sc in ring; do not join. (8 sc) Place marker to indicate beginning of rnd.

Note: Loop a short piece of yarn around any stitch to mark Rnd 1 as right side. Move stitch marker up with each rnd.

Rnd 2: 2 sc in each st around. (16 sc)

Rnd 3: (Sc in next st, 2 sc in next st) around. (24 sc)

Rnd 4: (Sc in next 2 sts, 2 sc in next st) around. (32 sc)

Rnd 5: (Sc in next 3 sts, 2 sc in next st) around. (40 sc)

Rnd 6: (Sc in next 4 sts, 2 sc in next st) around. (48 sc)

Rnd 7: (Sc in next 5 sts, 2 sc in next st) around. (56 sc)

Rnd 8: (Sc in next 6 sts, 2 sc in next st) around. (64 sc)

Rnd 9: (Sc in next 7 sts, 2 sc in next st) around. (72 sc)

Rnd 10: (Sc in next 8 sts, 2 sc in next st) around. (80 sc)

Rnd 11: Sc in each st around.

Rnd 12: (Sc in next 9 sts, 2 sc in next st) around. (88 sc)

Rnd 13: (Sc in next 10 sts, 2 sc in next st) around. (96 sc)

Rnd 14: Sc in each st around.

Rnd 15: (Sc in next 11 sts, 2 sc in next st) around. (104 sc)

Rnd 16: (Sc in next 12 sts, 2 sc in next st) around. (112 sc)

Rnd 17: Sc in each st around.

Rnd 18: (Sc in next 13 sts, 2 sc in next st) around. (120 sc)

Rnd 19: (Sc in next 14 sts, 2 sc in next st) around. (128 sc)

Rnds 20–24: Sc in each st around.

Rnd 25: (Sc in next 14 sts, sc2tog) around. (120 sc)

Rnd 26: Sc in each st around.

Rnd 27: (Sc in next 13 sts, sc2tog) around. (112 sc)

Rnd 28: Sc in each st around.

Rnd 29: (Sc in next 12 sts, sc2tog) around. (104 sc)

Rnd 30: (Sc in next 11 sts, sc2tog) around. (96 sc)

Rnd 31: (Sc in next 10 sts, sc2tog) around. (88 sc)

Fasten off.

Back
Repeat Front Rnds 1–12.
Fasten off, leaving a long tail for sewing.

Eye (make 2)

Rnd 1 (RS): With **B**, create magic ring, 6 sc in ring; join with sl st to first sc. (6 sc)

Fasten off.

Note: Loop a short piece of yarn around any stitch to mark Rnd 1 as right side. Move stitch marker up with each rnd.

Rnd 2: Pull up a loop of **C** in any st, ch 1, 2 sc in each st around; do not join. (12 sc)

Rnd 3: (Sc in next st, 2 sc in next st) around; join with sl st to first sc. (18 sc)

Fasten off.

Rnd 4: Pull up a loop of **A** in any st, ch 1, (sc in next 2 sts, 2 sc in next st) around; join with sl st to first sc. (24 sc)

Rnd 5: Ch 1, working in the BLO, sc in each st around; join with sl st to first sc.

Rnd 6: Ch 1, sc in each st around; do not join. Place marker to indicate beginning of rnd.

Rnds 7–9: Sc in each st around.

Rnd 10: (Sc in next 2 sts, sc2tog) around. (18 sc)

Rnd 11: (Sc in next st, sc2tog) around. (12 sc)

Stuff firmly.

Rnd 12: (Sc2tog) 6 times. (6 sc)

Fasten off, leaving a long tail for sewing.

Thread long tail in yarn needle and close Rnd 12.

Trim

Pull up a loop of **A** in exposed front loop from Rnd 5, sl st in each st around; join with sl st to first st.

Fasten off.

Leg (make 6)

Rnd 1 (RS): With **A**, create magic ring, 4 sc in ring; do not join. (4 sc) Place marker to indicate beginning of rnd.

Note: Loop a short piece of yarn around any stitch to mark Rnd 1 as right side. Move stitch marker up with each rnd.

Rnd 2: (Sc in next st, 2 sc in next st) around. (6 sc)

Rnds 3–14: Sc in each st around.

Fasten off, leaving a long tail for sewing.

Do not stuff.

Pincer (make 2)

With **A**, ch 6; join with sl st to first ch to form a ring.

Rnd 1 (RS): Ch 1, sc in each ch; do not join. (6 sc) Place marker to indicate beginning of rnd.

Note: Loop a short piece of yarn around any stitch to mark Rnd 1 as right side. Move stitch marker up with each rnd.

Rnds 2–4: Sc in each st around.

Rnd 5: (Sc in next st, 2 sc in next st) around. (9 sc)

Rnd 6: (Sc in next 2 sts, 2 sc in next st) around. (12 sc)

Rnd 7: (Sc in next st, 2 sc in next st) around. (18 sc)

Rnd 8: (Sc in next 2 sts, 2 sc in next st) around. (24 sc)

Rnds 9–12: Sc in each st around. Do not fasten off.

Part 1: Small

Rnd 1: Sc in next 5 sts, sk 14 sts, sc in next 5 sts; do not join. (10 sc) Place marker to indicate beginning of rnd.

Note: Loop a short piece of yarn around any stitch to mark Rnd 1 as right side. Move stitch marker up with each rnd.

Rnds 2–3: Sc in each st around.

Rnd 4: (Sc2tog) 5 times. (5 sc)

Fasten off, leaving a long tail.

Thread long tail through yarn needle and close Rnd 4.

Stuff Pincer firmly.

Part 2: Large

Rnd 1: Pull up a loop of **A** in next unworked st of Rnd 12, ch 1, sc in next 14 sts; do not join. (14 sc) Place marker to indicate beginning of rnd.

Note: Loop a short piece of yarn around any stitch to mark Rnd 1 as right side. Move stitch marker up with each rnd.

Rnd 2: (Sc2tog, sc in next 5 sts) around. (12 sc)

Rnds 3–6: Sc in each st around.

Stuff Pincer firmly.

Rnd 7: (Sc2tog) 6 times. (6 sc)

Fasten off, leaving a long tail.

Thread long tail through yarn needle and close Rnd 7.

Assembly

Use photos as a guide.

With WS facing, sew Front and Back together, stuffing before closing.

Sew sides of Eyes together firmly.

Sew joined Eyes to Body.

Sew Legs on Rnd 23 on Body.

Sew Pincers on each side of Body.

Happy the Platypus

Look at this supersize platypus, and I dare you to not smile. You can't do it! I can't! He makes me happy, and you'll make your little ones happy when they have a friendly platypus crochet friend who is as long as their leg.

Yarn
Valley Yarns Valley Superwash Super Bulky; super bulky #6; 100% extra fine superwash merino wool; 3.5 oz (100 g)/55 yd (50 m) per skein
- 5 skeins: 201 Aqua Oasis (**A**)
- 3 skeins: 002 Tan (**B**)

Hook and Other Materials
- US size J-10 (6 mm) crochet hook
- Yarn needle
- Poly-fil stuffing
- Two 15 mm safety eyes
- Stitch markers

Finished Measurement
About 27 in (68.5 cm), including tail

Gauge
11 sc and 11 rows/rounds = 4 in (10 cm)

Special Stitch
Invisible single crochet 2 together (sc2tog): Insert hook in the FLO of next 2 sts, yarn over and draw through both sts, yarn over and draw through 2 loops on hook (1 stitch decreased).

Pattern Note
Platypus is made in 6 pieces: Body, 4 Feet, and Tail.

INSTRUCTIONS

Body

Rnd 1 (RS): With **A**, create magic ring, 8 sc in ring; do not join. (8 sc) Place marker to indicate beginning of Rnd.

Note: Loop a short piece of yarn around any stitch to mark Rnd 1 as right side. Move stitch marker up with each rnd.

Rnd 2: 2 sc in each st around. (16 sc)

Rnd 3: (Sc in next st, 2 sc in next st) around. (24 sc)

Rnd 4: (Sc in next 2 sts, 2 sc in next st) around. (32 sc)

Rnd 5: (Sc in next 3 sts, 2 sc in next st) around. (40 sc)

Rnd 6: (Sc in next 4 sts, 2 sc in next st) around. (48 sc)

Rnd 7: (Sc in next 5 sts, 2 sc in next st) around. (56 sc)

Rnd 8: Sc in each st around.

Rnd 9: (Sc in next 6 sts, 2 sc in next st) around. (64 sc)

Rnds 10–22: Sc in each st around.

Rnd 23: (Sc in next 14 sts, sc2tog) around. (60 sc)

Rnd 24: Sc in each st around.

Rnd 25: (Sc in next 8 sts, sc2tog) around. (54 sc)

Rnds 26–28: Sc in each st around.

Rnd 29: (Sc in next 7 sts, sc2tog) around. (48 sc)

Rnds 30–32: Sc in each st around.

Rnd 33: (Sc in next 6 sts, sc2tog) around. (42 sc)

Rnds 34–35: Sc in each st around.

Rnd 36: (Sc in next 5 sts, sc2tog) around. (36 sc)

Rnds 37–38: Sc in each st around.

Rnd 39: (Sc in next 4 sts, sc2tog) around. (30 sc)

Rnd 40: Sc in each st around.

Rnd 41: (Sc in next 3 sts, sc2tog) around. (24 sc)
Stuff Body firmly.

Head

Rnd 42: (Sc in next 2 sts, 2 sc in next st) around. (32 sc)

Rnd 43: (Sc in next 3 sts, 2 sc in next st) around. (40 sc)

Rnd 44: (Sc in next 4 sts, 2 sc in next st) around. (48 sc)

Rnds 45–54: Sc in each st around.

Rnd 55: (Sc in next 4 sts, sc2tog) around. (40 sc)

Rnd 56: (Sc in next 3 sts, sc2tog) around. (32 sc)
Join **B**, fasten off **A**.

Bill

Rnd 57: Sc in each st around.

Rnd 58: (Sc in next 6 sts, sc2tog) around. (28 sc)

Rnd 59: (Sc in next 5 sts, sc2tog) around. (24 sc)

Rnd 60: (Sc in next 4 sts, sc2tog) around. (20 sc)

Rnd 61: (Sc in next 3 sts, sc2tog) around. (16 sc)

Rnds 62–64: Sc in each st around.

Stuff Head firmly.

Add safety eyes between Rnds 55 and 56 about 6 sts apart.

Rnd 65: (Sc in next 3 sts, 2 sc in next st) around. (20 sc)

Rnd 66: Sc in each st around.

Rnd 67: (Sc in next 4 sts, 2 sc in next st) around. (24 sc)

Rnd 68: Sc in each st around.

Rnd 69: (Sc in next 5 sts, 2 sc in next st) around. (28 sc)

Rnd 70: (Sc in next 6 sts, 2 sc in next st) around. (32 sc)

Rnd 71: (Sc in next 6 sts, sc2tog) around; join with sl st to first sc. (28 sc)

Fasten off.

Fold Bill in half in line with eyes and sew flat.

Foot (make 4)

With **B**, ch 12; join with sl st to first ch to form a ring.

Rnd 1 (RS): Ch 1, sc 12 in ring; do not join. (12 sc) Place stitch marker to indicate beginning of rnd.

Note: Loop a short piece of yarn around any stitch to mark Rnd 1 as right side. Move stitch marker up with each rnd.

Rnd 2: (Sc in next 2 sts, 2 sc in next st) around. (16 sc)

Rnd 3: Sc in each st around.

Rnd 4: (Sc in next 3 sts, 2 sc in next st) around. (20 sc)

Rnd 5: Sc in each st around.

Rnd 6: (Sc in next 4 sts, 2 sc in next st) around. (24 sc)

Rnd 7: (Sc in next 5 sts, 2 sc in next st) around. (28 sc)

Rnd 8: (Sc in next 5 sts, sc2tog) around. (24 sc)

Fasten off.

Fold in half and sew Rnd 8 together.

Stuff lightly.

Tail

Rnd 1 (RS): With **B**, create magic ring, 6 sc in ring; do not join. (6 sc) Place stitch marker to indicate beginning of rnd.

Note: Loop a short piece of yarn around any stitch to mark Rnd 1 as right side. Move stitch marker up with each rnd.

Rnd 2: 2 sc in each st around. (12 sc)

Rnd 3: Sc in each st around.

Rnd 4: (Sc in next st, 2 sc in next st) around. (18 sc)

Rnd 5: (Sc in next 2 sts, 2 sc in next st) around. (24 sc)

Rnd 6: (Sc in next 3 sts, 2 sc in next st) around. (30 sc)

Rnd 7: (Sc in next 4 sts, 2 sc in next st) around. (36 sc)

Rnd 8: (Sc in next 5 sts, 2 sc in next st) around. (42 sc)

Rnds 9–12: Sc in each st around.

Rnd 13: (Sc in next 5 sts, sc2tog) around. (36 sc)

Rnds 14–15: Sc in each st around.

Rnd 16: (Sc in next 4 sts, sc2tog) around. (30 sc)

Rnds 17–18: Sc in each st around.

Rnd 19: (Sc in next 3 sts, sc2tog) around. (24 sc)

Rnd 20: Sc in each st around.

Rnd 21: (Sc in next 2 sts, sc2tog) around. (18 sc)

Rnds 22–23: Sc in each st around.

Rnd 24: (Sc in next st, sc2tog) around. (12 sc)

Fasten off, leaving a long tail for sewing.

Assembly

Use photos as a guide

Sew Feet on Body.

Sew Tail on end of Body.

Chubb-Bee

Its name says it all, honey: "Chubb-Bee"! He's the chunkiest bee you'll find, and he's super-easy to crochet! Your hook will "fly" through this pattern, and your nest will be humming with lots of bees before you know it.

Yarn
Premier Yarns Parfait Chunky; super bulky #6; 100% superwash merino; 3.5 oz (100 g)/131 yd (120 m) per skein

- 2 skeins: 1150-12 Sunshine (**A**)
- 1 skein each: 1150-42 Espresso (**B**) and 1150-01 White (**C**)

Hook and Other Materials
- US size J-10 (6 mm) crochet hook
- Yarn needle
- Poly-fil stuffing
- Two 15 mm safety eyes
- Stitch markers

Finished Measurement
About 17 in (43 cm) long

Gauge
11 sc and 11 rows/rounds = 4 in (10 cm)

Special Stitch
Invisible single crochet 2 together (sc2tog): Insert hook in the FLO of next 2 sts, yarn over and draw through both sts, yarn over and draw through 2 loops on hook (1 stitch decreased).

Pattern Note
The bee is made in 3 parts: Body and 2 Wings. Details will be added with yarn needle to finish.

INSTRUCTIONS

Body

Rnd 1 (RS): With **A**, create magic ring, 8 sc in ring; do not join. (8 sc) Place stitch marker to indicate beginning of rnd.

Note: Loop a short piece of yarn around any stitch to mark Rnd 1 as right side. Move stitch marker up with each rnd.

Rnd 2: 2 sc in each st around. (16 sc)

Rnd 3: (Sc in next st, 2 sc in next st) around. (24 sc)

Rnd 4: (Sc in next 2 sts, 2 sc in next st) around. (32 sc)

Rnd 5: (Sc in next 3 sts, 2 sc in next st) around. (40 sc)

Rnd 6: (Sc in next 4 sts, 2 sc in next st) around. (48 sc)

Rnd 7: (Sc in next 5 sts, 2 sc in next st) around. (56 sc)

Rnd 8: (Sc in next 6 sts, 2 sc in next st) around. (64 sc)

Rnd 9: (Sc in next 7 sts, 2 sc in next st) around. (72 sc)

Rnds 10–22: Sc in each st around.

Join **B**, fasten off **A**.

Rnds 23–28: Sc in each st around.

Join **A**, fasten off **B**.

Rnds 29–34: Sc in each st around.

Join **B**, fasten off **A**.

Rnds 35–40: Sc in each st around.

Join **A**, fasten off **B**.

Rnds 41–46: Sc in each st around.

Join **B**, fasten off **A**.

Rnd 47: Sc in each st around.

Rnd 48: (Sc2tog, sc in next 34 sts) around. (70 sc)

Rnd 49: (Sc in next 5 sts, sc2tog) around. (60 sc)

Rnd 50: (Sc in next 4 sts, sc2tog) around. (50 sc)

Rnd 51: (Sc in next 3 sts, sc2tog) around. (40 sc)

Stuff Body firmly.

Add safety eyes between Rnds 5 and 6 about 12 sts apart.

Rnd 52: (Sc in next 2 sts, sc2tog) around. (30 sc)

Rnd 53: (Sc in next st, sc2tog) around. (20 sc)

Rnd 54: Sc2tog 10 times. (10 sc)

Rnd 55: Sc in each st around.

Rnd 56: Sc2tog, sc in next 8 sts. (9 sc)

Rnd 57: Sc in each st around.

Rnd 58: Sc2tog, sc in next 7 sts. (8 sc)

Rnd 59: Sc2tog 4 times. (4 sc)

Rnd 60: Sc2tog 2 times. (2 sc)

Fasten off, leaving a long tail for sewing.

Sew Rnd 60 closed.

Wing (make 2)

Rnd 1 (RS): With **C**, create magic ring, 8 sc in ring; do not join. (8 sc) Place stitch marker to indicate beginning of rnd.

Note: Loop a short piece of yarn around any stitch to mark Rnd 1 as right side. Move stitch marker up with each rnd.

Rnd 2: 2 sc in each st around. (16 sc)

Rnd 3: (Sc in next st, 2 sc in next st) around. (24 sc)

Rnd 4: (Sc in next 2 sts, 2 sc in next st) around. (32 sc)

Rnd 5: (Sc in next 3 sts, 2 sc in next st) around. (40 sc)

Rnds 6–13: Sc in each st around.

Rnd 14: (Sc in next 3 sts, sc2tog) around. (32 sc)

Rnd 15: Sc in each st around.

Rnd 16: (Sc in next 2 sts, sc2tog) around. (24 sc)

Rnd 17: (Sc in next st, sc2tog) around. (16 sc)

Fasten off, leaving a long tail for sewing.

Assembly

Use photos as a guide.

Sew Wings together and then onto Body.

Finishing

Join **B** on Rnd 11 above eye with sl st, ch 6, fasten off. Weave in ends. Repeat above 2nd eye.

Use yarn needle and **B** to stitch on eyebrows and mouth.

Skill Level: Easy

Shelby the Sheep

Crochet a new four-legged, furry friend whom you can really count on! This dreamy wool sheep is so cute and fuzzy, and it works up fast.

Yarn

Lion Brand Yarns Go For Faux Thick & Quick; jumbo weight #7; 100% polyester; 4.2 oz (120 g)/24 yd (22 m) per skein
- 8 skeins: 323-098 Baked Alaska (**A**)

Cascade Yarns Cherub Bulky; super bulky #6; 55% nylon/45% acrylic; 7.05 oz (200 g)/131 yd (120 m) per skein
- 2 skeins: 17 Steel Grey (**B**)

Hooks and Other Materials

- US size J-10 (6 mm) crochet hook
- US size N-13 (9 mm) crochet hook
- Yarn needle
- Poly-fil stuffing
- Two 15 mm safety eyes
- Stitch markers

Finished Measurement

About 14 in (35.5 cm) wide

Gauge

With **B** and smaller hook, 11 sc and 11 rows/rounds = 4 in (10 cm)

Special Stitch

Invisible single crochet 2 together (sc2tog): Insert hook in the FLO of next 2 sts, yarn over and draw through both sts, yarn over and draw through 2 loops on hook (1 stitch decreased).

Pattern Notes

- Sheep is made in 8 pieces: Body, Head, 2 Ears, and 4 Feet.
- This amigurumi is primarily made with a jumbo #7 yarn, but crocheting a mini with medium weight #4 yarn will not convert to similar proportions.

INSTRUCTIONS

Body

Rnd 1 (RS): With larger hook and **A**, beg at back end of Body, create magic ring, 8 sc in ring; do not join. (8 sc) Place marker to indicate beginning of rnd.

Note: Loop a short piece of yarn around any stitch to mark Rnd 1 as right side. Move stitch marker up with each rnd.

Rnd 2: 2 sc in each st around. (16 sc)

Rnd 3: (Sc in next st, 2 sc in next st) around. (24 sc)

Rnd 4: (Sc in next 2 sts, 2 sc in next st) around. (32 sc)

Rnd 5: (Sc in next 3 sts, 2 sc in next st) around. (40 sc)

Rnd 6: (Sc in next 4 sts, 2 sc in next st) around. (48 sc)

Rnds 7–18: Sc in each st around.

Rnd 19: (Sc in next 7 sts, sk next st) around. (42 sc)

Rnd 20: (Sc in next 6 sts, sk next st) around. (36 sc)

Rnd 21: (Sc in next 5 sts, sk next st) around. (30 sc)

Rnd 22: (Sc in next 4 sts, sk next st) around. (24 sc)

Rnd 23: (Sc in next 3 sts, sk next st) around. (18 sc)

Stuff body firmly.

Rnd 24: (Sc in next st, sk next st) around. (9 sc)

Fasten off, leaving a long tail for sewing.

Sew Rnd 24 closed.

Head

With **B** and smaller hook, ch 15.

Rnd 1 (RS): Sc in 2nd ch from hook and in next 12 chs, 3 sc in last ch, working on opposite side of chain, sc in next 12 chs, 2 sc in next st; do not join. (30 sc) Place marker to indicate beginning of rnd.

Note: Loop a short piece of yarn around any stitch to mark Rnd 1 as right side. Move stitch marker up with each rnd.

Rnd 2: 2 sc in next st, sc in next 12 sts, 2 sc in next 3 sts, sc in next 12 sts, 2 sc in next 2 sts. (36 sc)

Rnd 3: Sc in next st, 2 sc in next st, sc in next 12 sts, (sc in next st, 2 sc in next st) 3 times, sc in next 12 sts, (sc in next st, 2 sc in next st) 2 times. (42 sc)

Rnds 4–11: Sc in each st around.

Rnd 12: Sc in next st, sc2tog, sc in next 12 sts, sc2tog, sc in next 5 sts, sc2tog, sc in next 12 sts, sc2tog, sc in next 4 sts. (38 sc)

Rnds 13–18: Sc in each st around.

Fasten off.

Rnd 19: With larger hook, join **A** in any st, ch 1, (sc in next st, sk 1 st) around. (19 sts)

Rnd 20: Sc in each st around; join with a sl st to first st.

Fasten off, leaving a long end for sewing.

Add eyes between Rnds 14 and 15 about 4 sts apart.

Use yarn needle and long end to sew Rnd 20 straight across, stuffing before closing.

Ear (make 2)

Rnd 1 (RS): With smaller hook and **B**, create magic ring, 4 sc in ring; do not join. (4 sc) Place marker to indicate beginning of rnd.

Note: Loop a short piece of yarn around any stitch to mark Rnd 1 as right side. Move stitch marker up with each rnd.

Rnd 2: 2 sc in each st around. (8 sc)

Rnd 3: Sc in each st around.

Rnd 4: (Sc in next st, 2 sc in next st) around. (12 sc)

Rnd 5: (Sc in next 2 sts, 2 sc in next st) around. (16 sc)

Rnds 6–7: Sc in each st around.

Rnd 8: (Sc in next 2 sts, sc2tog) around. (12 sc)

Rnd 9: Sc in each st around.

Rnd 10: (Sc in next st, sc2tog) around. (8 sc)

Rnd 11: Sc in each st around.

Fasten off, leaving a long tail for sewing.

Feet (make 4)

Rnd 1 (RS): With smaller hook and **B**, create magic ring, 6 sc in ring; do not join. (6 sc) Place marker to indicate beginning of rnd.

Note: Loop a short piece of yarn around any stitch to mark Rnd 1 as right side. Move stitch marker up with each rnd.

Rnd 2: 2 sc in each st around. (12 sc)

Rnd 3: (Sc in next st, 2 sc in next st) around. (18 sc)

Rnd 4: (Sc in next 2 sts, 2 sc in next st) around. (24 sc)

Rnds 5–6: Sc in each st around.

Rnd 7: (Sc in next 2 sts, sc2tog) around. (18 sc)

Rnd 8: Sc in each st around.

Rnd 9: (Sc in next st, sc2tog) around. (12 sc)

Rnd 10: Sc in each st around.

Fasten off, leaving a long tail for sewing.

Assembly

Use photos as a guide.
Sew Ears on Head.
Sew Head on Body.
Stuff Legs firmly and sew on Body.

Denton the Woolly Mammoth

This supersize stuffed animal might not weigh 6 tons, but he is still larger than life! His fluffy body, trunk, and cool tusks make him one unusual amigurumi!

Yarn

Lion Brand Yarns Go For Faux Thick & Quick; super bulky weight #6; 100% polyester; 3.5 oz (100 g)/65 yd (60 m) per skein
- 4 skeins: 322-203 Pomeranian (**A**)

Lion Brand Yarns Wool-Ease Thick & Quick; super bulky weight #6; 80% acrylic/20% wool; 6 oz (170 g)/106 yd (97 m) per skein
- 4 skeins: 640-127 Peanut (**B**)
- 1 skein: 640-99 Fisherman (**C**)

Hooks and Other Materials
- US size J-10 (6 mm) crochet hook
- US size N-13 (9 mm) crochet hook
- Yarn needle
- Poly-fil stuffing
- Two 15 mm safety eyes
- Stitch markers

Finished Measurement
Sitting: About 21 in (53 cm) tall

Gauge
With **B** and smaller hook, 11 sc and 11 rows/rounds = 4 in (10 cm)

Special Stitch
Invisible single crochet 2 together (sc2tog): Insert hook in the FLO of next 2 sts, yarn over and draw through both sts, yarn over and draw through 2 loops on hook (1 stitch decreased).

Pattern Note
Mammoth is made in 11 pieces: Body, Head, 2 Ears, 2 Arms, 2 Legs, 2 Tusks, and 1 Trunk.

INSTRUCTIONS

Body

Rnd 1 (RS): With larger hook and **A**, create magic ring, 6 sc in ring; do not join. (6 sc) Place marker to indicate beginning of rnd.

Note: Loop a short piece of yarn around any stitch to mark Rnd 1 as right side. Move stitch marker up with each rnd.

Rnd 2: 2 sc in each st around. (12 sc)

Rnd 3: (Sc in next st, 2 sc in next st) around. (18 sc)

Rnd 4: (Sc in next 2 sts, 2 sc in next st) around. (24 sc)

Rnd 5: (Sc in next 3 sts, 2 sc in next st) around. (30 sc)

Rnd 6: (Sc in next 4 sts, 2 sc in next st) around. (36 sc)

Rnd 7: (Sc in next 5 sts, 2 sc in next st) around. (42 sc)

Rnd 8: (Sc in next 6 sts, 2 sc in next st) around. (48 sc)

Rnd 9: (Sc in next 7 sts, 2 sc in next st) around. (54 sc)

Rnds 10–20: Sc in each st around.

Rnd 21: (Sc in next 7 sts, sc2tog) around. (48 sc)

Rnds 22–23: Sc in each st around.

Rnd 24: (Sc in next 6 sts, sc2tog) around. (42 sc)

Rnds 25–26: Sc in each st around.

Rnd 27: (Sc in next 5 sts, sc2tog) around. (36 sc)

Rnds 28–29: Sc in each st around.

Rnd 30: (Sc in next 4 sts, sc2tog) around. (30 sc)

Rnd 31: (Sc in next 3 sts, sc2tog) around. (24 sc)

Rnd 32: (Sc in next 2 sts, sc2tog) around. (18 sc)

Stuff Body firmly.

Head

Rnd 33: 2 sc in each st around. (36 sc)

Rnd 34: Sc in each st around.

Rnd 35: (Sc in next 5 sts, 2 sc in next st) around. (42 sc)

Rnd 36: Sc in each st around.

Rnd 37: (Sc in next 6 sts, 2 sc in next st) around. (48 sc)

Rnds 38–39: Sc in each st around.

Rnd 40: (Sc in next 6 sts, sc2tog) around. (42 sc)

Rnd 41: Sc in each st around.

Rnd 42: (Sc in next 5 sts, sc2tog) around. (36 sc)

Rnds 43–44: Sc in each st around.

Rnd 45: (Sc in next 4 sts, sc2tog) around. (30 sc)

Rnd 46: (Sc in next 3 sts, sc2tog) around. (24 sc)

Stuff Head firmly.

Add eyes between Rnds 38 and 39 about 6 sts apart.

Rnd 47: (Sc in next 2 sts, sc2tog) around. (18 sc)

Rnd 48: (Sc in next st, sc2tog) around. (12 sc)

Rnd 49: (Sc2tog) 6 times. (6 sc)

Fasten off, leaving a long tail for sewing.

Use yarn needle and long tail to sew Rnd 49 closed.

Trunk

With smaller hook and **B**, ch 12; join to create a ring.

Note: Loop a short piece of yarn around any stitch to mark Rnd 1 as right side. Move stitch marker up with each rnd.

Rnd 1: Ch 1, 12 sc in ring; do not join. Place marker to indicate beginning of rnd.

Rnds 2–14: Sc in each st around.

Rnd 15: (Sc in next st, 2 sc in next st) around. (18 sc)

DENTON THE WOOLLY MAMMOTH

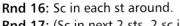

Rnd 16: Sc in each st around.

Rnd 17: (Sc in next 2 sts, 2 sc in next st) around.
(24 sc)

Fasten off, leaving a long tail for sewing.

Fold and sew Rnd 1 to Rnd 10.

Stuff the open end of Trunk.

Ear (make 2)

Row 1 (RS): With larger hook and **B**, create magic ring, 6 sc in ring; do not join. (6 sc) Place marker to indicate beginning of row.

Note: Loop a short piece of yarn around any stitch to mark Row 1 as right side. Move stitch marker up with each row.

Row 2: Ch 1, sc in next 2 sts, 2 sc in next 2 sts, sc in next 2 sts, turn. (8 sc)

Row 3: Ch 1, sc in next 3 sts, 2 sc in next 2 sts, sc in next 3 sts, turn. (10 sc)

Row 4: Ch 1, sc in next 2 sts, (2 sc in next st, sc in next 2 sts) two times, sc in next 2 sts, turn. (12 sc)

Row 5: Ch 1, sc in next 2 sts, (2 sc in next st, sc in next 3 sts) two times, sc in next 2 sts, turn. (14 sc)

Row 6: Ch 3 (counts as first dc), dc in next 3 sts, 3 dc in next st, dc in next 4 sts, 3 dc in next st, dc in next 4 sts, turn. (18 dc)

Row 7: Ch 1, sc in next 5 sts, 3 sc in next st, sc in next 6 sts, 3 sc in next st, sc in next 5 sts, turn. (22 sc)

Row 8: Ch 3 (counts as first dc), turn, dc in next 3 sts, turn. (4 dc)

Row 9: Ch 1, sc in next 4 sts, turn.

Row 10: Ch 1, sc in next 2 sts, sc2tog, turn. (3 sc)

Row 11: Ch 1, sc2tog, sc in next st. (2 sc)

Fasten off, leaving a long tail for sewing.

Use yarn needle and **A** to wrap around ends of stitches around the outside of each Ear for detail.

Tusk (make 2)

Rnd 1: With smaller hook and **C**, create magic ring, 3 sc in ring; do not join. (3 sc) Place marker to indicate beginning of rnd.

Note: Loop a short piece of yarn around any stitch to mark Rnd 1 as right side. Move stitch marker up with each rnd.

Rnd 2: 2 sc in each st around. (6 sc)

Rnd 3: Sc in each st around.

Rnd 4: (Sc in next st, 2 sc in next st) around. (9 sc)

Rnd 5: Sc in each st around.

Rnd 6: (Sc in next 2 sts, 2 sc in next st) around. (12 sc)

Rnd 7: Sc in each st around.

Fasten off, leaving a long tail for sewing.

Stuff loosely, leaving tip of Tusk empty.

Arm (make 2)

Rnd 1 (RS): With smaller hook and **B**, create magic ring, 6 sc in ring; do not join. (6 sc) Place marker to indicate beginning of rnd.

Note: Loop a short piece of yarn around any stitch to mark Rnd 1 as right side. Move stitch marker up with each rnd.

Rnd 2: 2 sc in each st around. (12 sc)

Rnd 3: (Sc in next st, 2 sc in next st) around. (18 sc)

Rnd 4: (Sc in next 2 sts, 2 sc in next st) around. (24 sc)

Fasten off **B**.

Rnd 5: With larger hook and **A**, join in any st, ch 1, sc in same st as joining, sk 1 st, (sc in next st, sk 1 st) around; do not join. (12 sc)

Rnds 6–18: Sc in each st around.

Fasten off, leaving a long tail for sewing.

Stuff end of Arm firmly, leaving remainder of Arm unstuffed.

Leg (make 2)

Rnd 1 (RS): With smaller hook and **B**, create magic ring, 7 sc in ring; do not join. (7 sc) Place marker to indicate beginning of rnd.

Note: Loop a short piece of yarn around any stitch to mark Rnd 1 as right side. Move stitch marker up with each rnd.

Rnd 2: 2 sc in each st around. (14 sc)

Rnd 3: (Sc in next st, 2 sc in next st) around. (21 sc)

Rnd 4: (Sc in next 2 sts, 2 sc in next st) around. (28 sc)

Fasten off **B**.

Rnd 5: With larger hook and **A**, join in any st, ch 1, sc in same st as joining, sk 1 st, (sc in next st, sk 1 st) around; do not join. (14 sc)

Rnds 6–18: Sc in each st around.

Fasten off, leaving a long tail for sewing.

Stuff end of Leg firmly, leaving remainder of Leg unstuffed.

Assembly

Use photos as a guide.

Sew Ears on each side of Head.

Sew Trunk about 3 rows below eyes.

Sew 1 Tusk on each side of Trunk.

Sew Arms and Legs on Body.

Floppy the Frog

The world's largest frog is called the Goliath Frog (found in West Africa). It can grow up to 15 inches, and I think Floppy the Frog might be from that family! My favorite parts are the supersize eyes and the tongue that is ready to catch that pesky bug!

Yarn

Yarnspirations Bernat Baby Blanket; super bulky weight #6; 100% polyester; 10.5 oz (300 g)/220 yd (201 m) per skein

- 3 skeins: 04801 Misty Jungle (**A**)
- 1 skein each: 04008 Vanilla (**B**), 02300 Baby Pink (tongue only) (**C**)

Hook and Other Materials

- US size J-10 (6 mm) crochet hook
- Yarn needle
- Poly-fil stuffing
- Two 15 mm safety eyes
- Stitch markers

Finished Measurement

About 19 in (48 cm) tall

Gauge

11 sc and 11 rows/rounds = 4 in (10 cm)

Special Stitch

Invisible single crochet 2 together (sc2tog): Insert hook in the FLO of next 2 sts, yarn over and draw through both sts, yarn over and draw through 2 loops on hook (1 stitch decreased).

Pattern Note

Frog is made in 9 pieces: Body, Head, 2 Eyes, 2 Legs, 2 Arms, and Tongue.

INSTRUCTIONS

Body

Rnd 1 (RS): With **A**, create magic ring, 8 sc in ring; do not join. (8 sc) Place marker to indicate beginning of rnd.

Note: Loop a short piece of yarn around any stitch to mark Rnd 1 as right side. Move stitch marker up with each rnd.

Rnd 2: 2 sc in each st around. (16 sc)

Rnd 3: (Sc in next st, 2 sc in next st) around. (24 sc)

Rnd 4: (Sc in next 2 sts, 2 sc in next st) around. (32 sc)

Rnd 5: (Sc in next 3 sts, 2 sc in next st) around. (40 sc)

Rnd 6: (Sc in next 4 sts, 2 sc in next st) around. (48 sc)

Rnd 7: (Sc in next 5 sts, 2 sc in next st) around. (56 sc)

Rnd 8: (Sc in next 6 sts, 2 sc in next st) around. (64 sc)

Rnds 9–23: Sc in each st around.

Rnd 24: (Sc in next 6 sts, sc2tog) around. (56 sc)

Rnd 25: Sc in each st around.

Rnd 26: (Sc in next 5 sts, sc2tog) around. (48 sc)

Rnd 27: Sc in each st around.

Rnd 28: (Sc in next 4 sts, sc2tog) around. (40 sc)

Rnd 29: (Sc in next 3 sts, sc2tog) around. (32 sc)

Rnd 30: (Sc in next 2 sts, sc2tog) around. (24 sc)

Join **B**, fasten off **A**.

Stuff Body firmly.

Head

Rnd 31: 2 sc in each st around. (48 sc)

Rnd 32: (Sc in next 5 sts, 2 sc in next st) around. (56 sc)

Rnd 33: (Sc in next 6 sts, 2 sc in next st) around. (64 sc)

Rnds 34–37: Sc in each st around.

Join **A**, fasten off **B**.

Rnd 38: Hdc in each st around; join with sl st to first hdc.

Rnd 39: Ch 1, sc in 3rd loop in each st around; do not join.

Rnds 40–43: Sc in each st around.

Rnd 44: (Sc in next 6 sts, sc2tog) around. (56 sc)

Rnd 45: (Sc in next 5 sts, sc2tog) around. (48 sc)

Rnd 46: (Sc in next 4 sts, sc2tog) around. (40 sc)

Rnd 47: (Sc in next 3 sts, sc2tog) around. (32 sc)

Stuff Head firmly.

Rnd 48: (Sc in next 2 sts, sc2tog) around. (24 sc)

Rnd 49: (Sc in next st, sc2tog) around. (16 sc)

Rnd 50: (Sc2tog) 8 times. (8 sc)

Fasten off, leaving a long tail for sewing.

Use yarn needle and long tail and close Rnd 50.

Eye (make 2)

Back

With **A**, ch 4.

Rnd 1 (RS): 9 dc in 4th ch from hook; join with sl st to beg ch-4. (10 dc)

Rnd 2: Ch 3, dc in same st, 2 dc in each st around; join with sl st to beg ch-3. (20 dc)

Fasten off, leaving a long tail for sewing.

Front

Rnd 1 (RS): With **B**, create magic ring, 6 sc in ring; do not join. (6 sc) Place marker to indicate beginning of rnd.

Rnd 2: 2 sc in each st around.

Rnd 3: (Sc in next st, 2 sc in next st) around. (18 sc)

Rnd 4: Sc in each st around.

Fasten off, leaving a long tail for sewing.

Eye Assembly

Add safety eye on Rnd 1 outside of the center.

Use yarn needle to sew Front on the Back, stuffing before closing.

Leg (make 2)

With **A**, ch 18; join with sl st to first ch to form a ring.

Rnd 1: Ch 1, 18 sc in ring; do not join. (18 sc) Place marker to indicate beginning of rnd.

Rnds 2–18: Sc in each st around.

Rnd 19: Sc in next 2 sts, (sc 2, sc2tog) around. (14 sc)

Rnd 20: (Sc2tog) 7 times. (7 sc)

Rnd 21: Fold opening in half, work through both sides as one stitch to close opening as you go; *sl st in next st, ch 6, sl st in 4th ch from hook, sl st in next 2 chs, sl st in same st as first sl st; rep from * 2 more times; sl st to last st to finish.

Fasten off.

Use yarn needle to sew Rnd 1 to Rnd 15 to create a bend in the Leg.

Arm (make 2)

With **A**, ch 14; join with sl st to first ch to form a ring.

Rnd 1: Ch 1, 14 sc in ring; do not join. (14 sc) Place marker to indicate beginning of rnd.

Rnds 2–13: Sc in each st around.

Rnd 14: (Sc2tog) 7 times. (7 sc)

Rnd 15: Fold opening in half, work through both sides as one stitch to close opening as you go; *sl st in next st, ch 6, sl st in 4th ch from hook, sl st in next 2 chs, sl st in same st as first sl st; rep from * 2 more times; sl st to last st to finish.

Fasten off.

Tongue

With **C**, ch 6.

Row 1: Sc in 2nd ch from hook and in each ch across. (5 sc)

Rows 2–3: Turn, ch 1, sc in each st across.

Row 4: Sc2tog, sc in next st, sc2tog. (3 sc)

Fasten off.

Assembly
Use photos as a guide.
Sew Eyes on Head.
Sew Tongue on Head.
Sew Arms and Legs on Body.

Penny the Puppy

Penny the Puppy just wants to play! His floppy ears, kind eyes, and playful stitching will have you making your own puppy litter!

Yarn
Lion Brand Yarns Wool-Ease Thick & Quick; super bulky weight #6; 80% acrylic/20% wool; 6 oz (170 g)/106 yd (97 m) per skein
- 5 skeins: 640-542 Seaglass (**A**)
- 1 skein: 640-116 Succulent (**B**)

Hooks and Other Materials
- US size J-10 (6 mm) crochet hook
- Yarn needle
- Poly-fil stuffing
- Two 15 mm safety eyes
- Stitch markers

Finished Measurement
Sitting: About 18 in (45.5 cm) tall

Gauge
11 sc and 11 rows/rounds = 4 in (10 cm)

Special Stitch
Invisible single crochet 2 together (sc2tog): Insert hook in the FLO of next 2 sts, yarn over and draw through both sts, yarn over and draw through 2 loops on hook (1 stitch decreased).

Pattern Note
Puppy is made in 10 pieces: Head, Body, Nose, 2 Ears, Tail, 2 Legs, and 2 Arms.

INSTRUCTIONS

Body

Rnd 1 (RS): With **A**, create magic ring, 8 sc in ring; do not join. (8 sc) Place marker to indicate beginning of rnd.

Note: Loop a short piece of yarn around any stitch to mark Rnd 1 as right side. Move stitch marker up with each rnd.

Rnd 2: 2 sc in each st around. (16 sc)

Rnd 3: (Sc in next st, 2 sc in next st) around. (24 sc)

Rnd 4: (Sc in next 2 sts, 2 sc in next st) around. (32 sc)

Rnd 5: (Sc in next 3 sts, 2 sc in next st) around. (40 sc)

Rnd 6: (Sc in next 4 sts, 2 sc in next st) around. (48 sc)

Rnd 7: (Sc in next 5 sts, 2 sc in next st) around. (56 sc)

Rnd 8: (Sc in next 6 sts, 2 sc in next st) around. (64 sc)

Rnds 9–23: Sc in each st around.

Rnd 24: (Sc in next 6 sts, sc2tog) around. (56 sc)

Rnd 25–26: Sc in each st around.

Rnd 27: (Sc in next 5 sts, sc2tog) around. (48 sc)

Rnds 28–29: Sc in each st around.

Rnd 30: (Sc in next 4 sts, sc2tog) around. (40 sc)

Rnds 31–32: Sc in each st around.

Rnd 33: (Sc in next 3 sts, sc2tog) around. (32 sc)

Rnds 34–35: Sc in each st around.

Rnd 36: (Sc in next 2 sts, sc2tog) around. (24 sc)
Fasten off.
Stuff Body firmly.

Head

Rnd 1 (RS): With **A**, create magic ring, 6 sc in ring; do not join. (6 sc) Place marker to indicate beginning of rnd.

Note: Loop a short piece of yarn around any stitch to mark Rnd 1 as right side. Move stitch marker up with each rnd.

Rnd 2: 2 sc in each st around. (12 sc)

Rnd 3: (Sc in next st, 2 sc in next st) around. (18 sc)

Rnd 4: (Sc in next 2 sts, 2 sc in next st) around. (24 sc)

Rnd 5: (Sc in next 3 sts, 2 sc in next st) around. (30 sc)

Rnd 6: (Sc in next 4 sts, 2 sc in next st) around. (36 sc)

Rnds 7–8: Sc in each st around.

Rnd 9: (Sc in next 4 sts, sc2tog) around. (30 sc)

Rnd 10: Sc in each st around.

Rnd 11: (Sc in next 3 sts, sc2tog) around. (24 sc)

Rnd 12: Sc in each st around.

Rnd 13: (Sc in next 2 sts, sc2tog) around. (18 sc)

Rnd 14: 2 sc in each st around. (36 sc)

Rnd 15: (Sc in next 5 sts, 2 sc in next st) around. (42 sc)

Rnd 16: (Sc in next 6 sts, 2 sc in next st) around. (48 sc)

Rnd 17: (Sc in next 7 sts, 2 sc in next st) around. (54 sc)

Rnds 18–25: Sc in each st around.

Rnd 26: (Sc in next 7 sts, sc2tog) around. (48 sc)

Rnd 27: Sc in each st around.

Rnd 28: (Sc in next 6 sts, sc2tog) around. (42 sc)

Rnd 29: Sc in each st around.

Rnd 30: (Sc in next 5 sts, sc2tog) around. (36 sc)
Stuff Head firmly.
Add safety eyes between Rnds 16 and 17.

Rnd 31: (Sc in next 4 sts, sc2tog) around. (30 sc)

Rnd 32: (Sc in next 3 sts, sc2tog) around. (24 sc)

Rnd 33: (Sc in next 2 sts, sc2tog) around. (18 sc)

Rnd 34: (Sc in next st, sc2tog) around. (12 sc)

Rnd 35: (Sc2tog) 6 times. (6 sc)
Fasten off, leaving a long tail for sewing.
Use yarn needle and long tail to close Rnd 35.

Nose

Rnd 1 (RS): With **B**, create magic ring, 4 sc in ring; do not join. (4 sc) Place marker to indicate beginning of rnd.
Note: Loop a short piece of yarn around any stitch to mark Rnd 1 as right side. Move stitch marker up with each rnd.

Rnd 2: 2 sc in each st around. (8 sc)

Rnd 3: Sc in each st around; join with sl st to first sc.
Fasten off, leaving a long tail for sewing.

Tail

Rnd 1 (RS): With **B**, create magic ring, 4 sc in ring; do not join. (4 sc) Place marker to indicate beginning of rnd.
Note: Loop a short piece of yarn around any stitch to mark Rnd 1 as right side. Move stitch marker up with each rnd.

Rnds 2–12: Sc in each st around.
Fasten off, leaving a long tail for sewing.

Leg (make 2)

Rnd 1 (RS): With **B**, create magic ring, 6 sc in ring; do not join. (6 sc) Place marker to indicate beginning of rnd.
Note: Loop a short piece of yarn around any stitch to mark Rnd 1 as right side. Move stitch marker up with each rnd.

Rnd 2: 2 sc in each st around. (12 sc)

Rnd 3: (Sc in next st, 2 sc in next st) around. (18 sc)

Rnd 4: (Sc in next 2 sts, 2 sc in next st) around. (24 sc)
Fasten off **B**.

Rnd 5: Join **A** in BLO, ch 1, working in the BLO, sc in each st around; join with sl st to first sc.

Rnd 6: Ch 1, sc in each st around; do not join.

Rnds 7–10: Sc in each st around.

Rnd 11: (Sc in next 2 sts, sc2tog) around. (18 sc)

Rnds 12–23: Sc in each st around.
Fasten off, leaving a long tail for sewing.
Stuff Leg firmly at the paw section, leaving remaining unstuffed.

Arm (make 2)

Rnd 1 (RS): With **B**, create magic ring, 6 sc in ring; do not join. (6 sc) Place marker to indicate beginning of rnd.

Note: Loop a short piece of yarn around any stitch to mark Rnd 1 as right side. Move stitch marker up with each rnd.

Rnd 2: 2 sc in each st around. (12 sc)

Rnd 3: (Sc in next st, 2 sc in next st) around. (18 sc) Fasten off **B**.

Rnd 4: Join **A** in BLO, ch 1, working in the BLO, sc in each st around; join with sl st to first sc.

Rnd 5: Ch 1, sc in each st around; do not join.

Rnds 6–8: Sc in each st around.

Rnd 9: (Sc in next 7 sts, sc2tog) around. (16 sc)

Rnds 10–21: Sc in each st around.

Fasten off, leaving a long tail for sewing.

Stuff Arm firmly at the paw section, leaving remaining unstuffed.

Ear (make 2)

Rnd 1 (RS): With **B**, create magic ring, 6 sc in ring; do not join. (6 sc) Place marker to indicate beginning of rnd.

Note: Loop a short piece of yarn around any stitch to mark Rnd 1 as right side. Move stitch marker up with each rnd.

Rnd 2: 2 sc in each st around. (12 sc)

Rnd 3: (Sc in next st, 2 sc in next st) around. (18 sc)

Rnd 4: (Sc in next 2 sts, 2 sc in next st) around. (24 sc)

Rnd 5: (Sc in next 3 sts, 2 sc in next st) around. (30 sc)

Rnds 6–9: Sc in each st around.

Rnd 10: (Sc in next 3 sts, sc2tog) around. (24 sc)

Rnds 11–13: Sc in each st around.

Rnd 14: (Sc in next 2 sts, sc2tog) around. (18 sc)

Rnds 15–17: Sc in each st around.

Rnd 18: (Sc in next st, sc2tog) around. (12 sc)

Rnd 19: Sc in each st around; join with sl st to first sc.

Fasten off, leaving a long tail for sewing.

Do not stuff.

Assembly

Use photos as a guide.

Sew Nose on end of snout, stuffing before closing.

Sew Ears on Head.

Sew Arms and Legs on Body.

Sew Tail on middle lower back of Body.

Finishing

Thread **B** in yarn needle and stitch on mouth below Nose.

Eddy the Raccoon

This adorable outlaw is ready for mischief! His infamous mask will bring out the ninja in any kid! The ringed tail is so cute. Make a mini for a night of fun!

Yarn

Valley Yarns Valley Superwash Super Bulky; super bulky weight #6; 100% extra fine superwash merino wool; 3.5 oz (100 g)/55 yd (50 m) per skein

- 8 skeins: 017 Steel Grey (**A**)
- 3 skeins: 19 Black (**B**)
- 1 skein: 001 Natural (**C**)

Hook and Other Materials

- US size J-10 (6 mm) crochet hook
- Yarn needle
- Poly-fil stuffing
- Two 15 mm safety eyes
- Stitch markers

Finished Measurement

About 18 in (45.5 cm) tall

Gauge

11 sc and 11 rows/rounds = 4 in (10 cm)

Special Stitch

Invisible single crochet 2 together (sc2tog): Insert hook in the FLO of next 2 sts, yarn over and draw through both sts, yarn over and draw through 2 loops on hook (1 stitch decreased).

Pattern Note

Racoon is made in 12 pieces: Body, Head, Nose, 2 Ears, 2 Eye Patches, Tail, 2 Legs, and 2 Arms.

INSTRUCTIONS

Body

Rnd 1 (RS): With **A**, create magic ring, 8 sc in ring; do not join. (8 sc) Place marker to indicate beginning of rnd.

Note: Loop a short piece of yarn around any stitch to mark Rnd 1 as right side. Move stitch marker up with each rnd.

Rnd 2: 2 sc in each st around. (16 sc)

Rnd 3: (Sc in next st, 2 sc in next st) around. (24 sc)

Rnd 4: (Sc in next 2 sts, 2 sc in next st) around. (32 sc)

Rnd 5: (Sc in next 3 sts, 2 sc in next st) around. (40 sc)

Rnd 6: (Sc in next 4 sts, 2 sc in next st) around. (48 sc)

Rnd 7: (Sc in next 5 sts, 2 sc in next st) around. (56 sc)

Rnd 8: (Sc in next 6 sts, 2 sc in next st) around. (64 sc)

Rnds 9–23: Sc in each st around.

Rnd 24: (Sc in next 6 sts, sc2tog) around. (56 sc)

Rnds 25–26: Sc in each st around.

Rnd 27: (Sc in next 5 sts, sc2tog) around. (48 sc)

Rnd 28: Sc in each st around.

Rnd 29: (Sc in next 4 sts, sc2tog) around. (40 sc)

Rnd 30: Sc in each st around.

Rnd 31: (Sc in next 3 sts, sc2tog) around. (32 sc)

Rnd 32: Sc in each st around.

Rnd 33: (Sc in next 2 sts, sc2tog) around. (24 sc)

Stuff Body firmly.

Head

Rnd 34: 2 sc in each st around. (48 sc)

Rnd 35: (Sc in next 5 sts, 2 sc in next st) around. (56 sc)

Rnd 36: (Sc in next 6 sts, 2 sc in next st) around. (64 sc)

Rnd 37: (Sc in next 7 sts, 2 sc in next st) around. (72 sc)

Rnds 38–40: Sc in each st around.

Rnd 41: (Sc in next 7 sts, sc2tog) around. (64 sc)

Rnd 42: Sc in each st around.

Rnd 43: (Sc in next 6 sts, sc2tog) around. (56 sc)

Rnd 44: Sc in each st around.

Rnd 45: (Sc in next 5 sts, sc2tog) around. (48 sc)

Rnd 46: Sc in each st around.

Rnd 47: (Sc in next 4 sts, sc2tog) around. (40 sc)

Rnds 48–50: Sc in each st around.

Rnd 51: (Sc in next 3 sts, sc2tog) around. (32 sc)

Stuff Head firmly.

Rnd 52: Sc in each st around.

Rnd 53: (Sc in next 2 sts, sc2tog) around. (24 sc)

Rnd 54: (Sc in next st, sc2tog) around. (16 sc)

Rnd 55: (Sc2tog) 8 times. (8 sc)

Fasten off, leaving a long tail for sewing.

Use yarn needle and long tail to close Rnd 55.

Nose

Rnd 1 (RS): With **C**, create magic ring, 6 sc in ring; do not join. (6 sc) Place marker to indicate beginning of rnd.

Note: Loop a short piece of yarn around any stitch to mark Rnd 1 as right side. Move stitch marker up with each rnd.

Rnd 2: Sc in each st around.

Rnd 3: 2 sc in each st around. (12 sc)

Rnd 4: (Sc in next st, 2 sc in next st) around. (18 sc)

Rnds 5–6: Sc in each st around; join with sl st to first sc.

Fasten off, leaving a long tail for sewing.

Join **B**, fasten off **A**.

Rnds 13–16: Sc in each st around.

Join **A**, fasten off **B**.

Rnds 17–19: Sc in each st around.

Rnd 20: (Sc in next 2 sts, sc2tog) around. (18 sc)

Rnds 21–23: Sc in each st around.

Stuff end of Tail firmly; leave last 2 in (5 cm) unstuffed.

Rnd 24: (Sc in next st, sc2tog) around. (12 sc)

Rnds 25–26: Sc in each st around; join with sl st to first sc.

Fasten off, leaving a long tail for sewing.

Eye Patch (make 2)

With **B**, ch 2.

Row 1: 3 sc in 2nd ch from hook.

Row 2: Ch 1, turn, 2 sc in first st, sc in next st, 2 sc in next st. (5 sc)

Tail

Rnd 1 (RS): With **B**, create magic ring, 4 sc in ring; do not join. (4 sc) Place marker to indicate beginning of rnd.

Note: Loop a short piece of yarn around any stitch to mark Rnd 1 as right side. Move stitch marker up with each rnd.

Rnd 2: (Sc in next st, 2 sc in next st) around. (6 sc)

Rnd 3: (Sc in next 2 sts, 2 sc in next st) around. (8 sc)

Rnd 4: (Sc in next 3 sts, 2 sc in next st) around. (10 sc)

Rnd 5: (Sc in next 4 sts, 2 sc in next st) around. (12 sc)

Rnd 6: (Sc in next st, 2 sc in next st) around. (18 sc)

Rnd 7: Sc in each st around.

Rnd 8: (Sc in next 2 sts, 2 sc in next st) around. (24 sc)

Join **A**, fasten off **B**.

Rnds 9–12: Sc in each st around.

Row 3: Ch 1, turn, 2 sc in first st, sc in next 3 sts, 2 sc in next st. (7 sc)

Row 4: Ch 1, turn, 2 sc in first st, sc in next 5 sts, 2 sc in next st. (9 sc)

Rows 5–7: Ch 1, turn, sc in each st across.

Join **C**, fasten off **B**.

Row 8: Ch 1, sc in each st across.

Fasten off, leaving a long tail for sewing.

Use photos as a guide and add safety eye on Eye Patch.

Ear (make 2)

Rnd 1 (RS): With **B**, create magic ring, 3 sc in ring; do not join. (3 sc) Place marker to indicate beginning of rnd.

Note: Loop a short piece of yarn around any stitch to mark Rnd 1 as right side. Move stitch marker up with each rnd.

Rnd 2: 2 sc in each st around. (6 sc)

Rnd 3: (Sc in next st, 2 sc in next st) around. (9 sc)

Rnd 4: (Sc in next 2 sts, 2 sc in next st) around. (12 sc)

Rnd 5: (Sc in next 3 sts, 2 sc in next st) around. (15 sc)

Rnd 6: Sc in each st around.

Rnd 7: (Sc in next 3 sts, sc2tog) around. (12 sc)

Fasten off, leaving a long tail for sewing.

Leg (make 2)

Rnd 1 (RS): With **B**, create magic ring, 6 sc in ring; do not join. (6 sc) Place marker to indicate beginning of rnd.

Note: Loop a short piece of yarn around any stitch to mark Rnd 1 as right side. Move stitch marker up with each rnd.

Rnd 2: 2 sc in each st around. (12 sc)

Rnd 3: (Sc in next st, 2 sc in next st) around. (18 sc)

Rnd 4: (Sc in next 2 sts, 2 sc in next st) around. (24 sc)

Rnd 5: (Sc in next 3 sts, 2 sc in next st) around. (30 sc)

Rnd 6: Sc in each st around.

Rnd 7: (Sc in next 3 sts, sc2tog) around. (24 sc)

Rnd 8: (Sc in next 2 sts, sc2tog) around. (18 sc)

Rnds 9–14: Sc in each st around.

Rnd 15: (Sc in next 7 sts, sc2tog) around. (16 sc)

Join **A**, fasten off **B**.

Rnds 16–23: Sc in each st around.

Fasten off, leaving a long tail for sewing.

Stuff firmly at paw section, lightly stuff Leg, and leave remaining 2½ in (6.4 cm) unstuffed.

Arm (make 2)

Rnd 1 (RS): With **B**, create magic ring, 6 sc in ring; do not join. (6 sc) Place marker to indicate beginning of rnd.

Note: Loop a short piece of yarn around any stitch to mark Rnd 1 as right side. Move stitch marker up with each rnd.

Rnd 2: 2 sc in each st around. (12 sc)

Rnd 3: (Sc in next st, 2 sc in next st) around. (18 sc)

Rnd 4: (Sc in next 2 sts, 2 sc in next st) around. (24 sc)

Rnd 5: Sc in each st around.

Rnd 6: (Sc in next 2 sts, sc2tog) around. (18 sc)

Rnd 7: (Sc in next 7 sts, sc2tog) around. (16 sc)

Rnds 8–12: Sc in each st around.

Join **A**, fasten off **B**.

Rnds 13–21: Sc in each st around.

Fasten off, leaving a long tail for sewing.

Stuff firmly at paw section, lightly stuff Arm, and leave remaining 2½ in (6.4 cm) unstuffed.

Assembly

Use photos as a guide.

Sew Nose on Head, stuffing before closing.

Sew Eye Patches on each side of Nose at an angle.

Sew Ears on Head.

Sew Arms and Legs on Body.

Sew Tail on lower middle back.

Finishing

Thread **B** in yarn needle and stitch detail on tip of nose.

Alton the Tiger

This amigurumi is the purr-fect addition to this supersize collection! The body is made with basic stitches, while the striping is just stitched on for detail.

Yarn

Cascade Yarns Cherub Bulky; super bulky weight #6; 55% nylon/45% acrylic; 7.05 oz (200 g)/ 131 yd (120 m) per skein

- 3 skeins: 99 Harvest Pumpkin (**A**)
- 1 skein each: 01 White (**B**), 40 Black (**C**)

Hook and Other Materials

- US size J-10 (6 mm) crochet hook
- Yarn needle
- Poly-fil stuffing
- Two 15 mm safety eyes
- Stitch markers

Finished Measurement

About 15.5 in (39.5 cm) high (not counting ears)

Gauge

11 sc and 11 rows/rounds = 4 in (10 cm)

Special Stitch

Invisible single crochet 2 together (sc2tog): Insert hook in the FLO of next 2 sts, yarn over and draw through both sts, yarn over and draw through 2 loops on hook (1 stitch decreased).

Pattern Note

Tiger is made in 11 pieces: Body, Head, Snout, 2 Arms, 2 Legs, 2 Ears, Tail, and Belly. It is finished by adding detailing stripes.

INSTRUCTIONS

Body

Rnd 1 (RS): With **A**, create magic ring, 8 sc in ring; do not join. (8 sc) Place marker to indicate beginning of rnd.

Note: Loop a short piece of yarn around any stitch to mark Rnd 1 as right side. Move stitch marker up with each rnd.

Rnd 2: 2 sc in each st around. (16 sc)

Rnd 3: (Sc in next st, 2 sc in next st) around. (24 sc)

Rnd 4: (Sc in next 2 sts, 2 sc in next st) around. (32 sc)

Rnd 5: (Sc in next 3 sts, 2 sc in next st) around. (40 sc)

Rnd 6: (Sc in next 4 sts, 2 sc in next st) around. (48 sc)

Rnd 7: (Sc in next 5 sts, 2 sc in next st) around. (56 sc)

Rnd 8: (Sc in next 6 sts, 2 sc in next st) around. (64 sc)

Rnds 9–30: Sc in each st around.

Rnd 31: (Sc in next 6 sts, sc2tog) around. (56 sc)

Rnd 32: Sc in each st around.

Rnd 33: (Sc in next 5 sts, sc2tog) around. (48 sc)

Rnd 34: Sc in each st around.

Rnd 35: (Sc in next 4 sts, sc2tog) around. (40 sc)

Rnd 36: (Sc in next 3 sts, sc2tog) around. (32 sc)

Rnd 37: (Sc in next 2 sts, sc2tog) around. (24 sc)

Stuff Body.

Head

Rnd 38: 2 sc in each st around. (48 sc)

Rnd 39: (Sc in next 5 sts, 2 sc in next st) around. (56 sc)

Rnd 40: (Sc in next 6 sts, 2 sc in next st) around. (64 sc)

Rnds 41–53: Sc in each st around.

Rnd 54: (Sc in next 6 sts, sc2tog) around. (56 sc)

Rnd 55: Sc in each st around.

Rnd 56: (Sc in next 5 sts, sc2tog) around. (48 sc)

Rnd 57: (Sc in next 4 sts, sc2tog) around. (40 sc)

Rnd 58: (Sc in next 3 sts, sc2tog) around. (32 sc)

Rnd 59: (Sc in next 2 sts, sc2tog) around. (24 sc)

Stuff Head.

Rnd 60: (Sc in next st, sc2tog) around. (16 sc)

Rnd 61: (Sc2tog) 8 times.

Fasten off, leaving a long tail.

Use yarn needle and long tail to sew Rnd 61 closed.

Leg (make 2)

Rnd 1 (RS): With **B**, create magic ring, 5 sc in ring; do not join. (5 sc) Place marker to indicate beginning of rnd.

Note: Loop a short piece of yarn around any stitch to mark Rnd 1 as right side. Move stitch marker up with each rnd.

Rnd 2: 2 sc in each st around. (10 sc)

Rnd 3: (Sc in next st, 2 sc in next st) around. (15 sc)

Rnd 4: (Sc in next 2 sts, 2 sc in next st) around. (20 sc)

Rnd 5: (Sc in next 3 sts, 2 sc in next st) around. (25 sc)

Rnd 6: Sc in each st around.

Fasten off.

Rnd 7: Join **A** in any st, ch 1, sc in next 23 sts, sc2tog around; do not join. (24 sc)

Rnd 8: (Sc in next 2 sts, sc2tog) around. (18 sc)

Rnds 9–14: Sc in each st around.

Rnd 15: (Sc in next 7 sts, sc2tog) around. (16 sc)

Rnds 16–23: Sc in each st around.

Fasten off, leaving a long tail for sewing.

Stuff firmly at paw section, lightly stuff Leg, and leave remaining 2½ in (6.4 cm) unstuffed.

Arm (make 2)

Rnd 1 (RS): With **B**, create magic ring, 5 sc in ring; do not join. (5 sc) Place marker to indicate beginning of rnd.

Note: Loop a short piece of yarn around any stitch to mark Rnd 1 as right side. Move stitch marker up with each rnd.

Rnd 2: 2 sc in each st around. (10 sc)

Rnd 3: (Sc in next st, 2 sc in next st) around. (15 sc)

Rnd 4: (Sc in next 2 sts, 2 sc in next st) around. (20 sc)

Rnd 5: Sc in each st around.

Fasten off.

Rnd 6: Join **A** in any st, ch 1, (sc in next 2 sts, sc2tog) around. (15 sc)

Rnds 7–22: Sc in each st around.

Fasten off, leaving a long tail for sewing.

Snout

Rnd 1 (RS): With **B**, create magic ring, 6 sc in ring; do not join. (6 sc) Place marker to indicate beginning of rnd.

Note: Loop a short piece of yarn around any stitch to mark Rnd 1 as right side. Move stitch marker up with each rnd.

Row 4: Ch 1, 2 sc in first st, sc in next 10 sts, 2 sc in next st, turn. (14 sc)

Row 5: Ch 1, sc in each st across, turn.

Row 6: Ch 1, 2 sc in first st, sc in next 12 sts, 2 sc in next st, turn. (16 sc)

Rows 7–12: Ch 1, sc in each st across, turn.

Row 13: Ch 1, sc2tog, sc in next 12 sts, sc2tog, turn. (14 sc)

Row 14: Ch 1, sc in each st across, turn.

Row 15: Ch 1, sc2tog, sc in next 10 sts, sc2tog, turn. (12 sc)

Row 16: Ch 1, sc in each st across, turn.

Row 17: Ch 1, sc2tog, sc in next 8 sts, sc2tog, turn. (10 sc)

Border

Rnd 1 (RS): Ch 1, sc2tog, sc in next 6 sts, sc2tog, sc 18 evenly down ends of rows, sc 10 across Row 1, sc 18 evenly down ends of rows; join with sl st to first sc. (54 sc)

Fasten off, leaving a long tail for sewing.

Ear (make 2)

Rnd 1 (RS): With **A**, create magic ring, 4 sc in ring; do not join. (4 sc) Place marker to indicate beginning of rnd.

Note: Loop a short piece of yarn around any stitch to mark Rnd 1 as right side. Move stitch marker up with each rnd.

Rnd 2: 2 sc in each st around. (8 sc)

Rnd 3: (Sc in next st, 2 sc in next st) around. (12 sc)

Rnds 4–5: Sc in each st around.

Fasten off, leaving a long tail for sewing.

Rnd 2: 2 sc in each st around. (12 sc)

Rnd 3: (Sc in next 3 sts, 2 sc in next st) around. (15 sc)

Rnd 4: (Sc in next 4 sts, 2 sc in next st) around. (18 sc)

Rnd 5: Sc in each st around.

Fasten off.

Belly

With **B**, ch 9.

Row 1 (WS): 2 sc in 2nd ch from hook, sc in next 6 chs, 2 sc in next ch, turn. (10 sc)

Row 2 (RS): Ch 1, 2 sc in first st, sc in next 8 sts, 2 sc in next st, turn. (12 sc)

Row 3: Ch 1, sc in each st across, turn.

Tail

Rnd 1 (RS): With **A**, create magic ring, 6 sc in ring; do not join. (6 sc) Place marker to indicate beginning of rnd.

Note: Loop a short piece of yarn around any stitch to mark Rnd 1 as right side. Move stitch marker up with each rnd. Stuff lightly as Tail progresses.

Rnds 2–25: Sc in each st around.

Fasten off, leaving a long tail for sewing.

Assembly

Use photos as a guide.

Sew Snout on Head, stuffing before closing.

With **C**, stitch nose on Snout.

Thread yarn needle with **B**, pinch the top of nose and stitch in place.

Sew Ears on Head.

Sew Arms and Legs on Body.

Sew Belly on Body.

Sew Tail on lower middle back.

Use photos as a guide and stitch on stripes.

Flutter the Butterfly

Out of all 20,000 butterfly species, this one is the biggest, at a whopping 16 inches! You'll love the sweetness this butterfly adds to the collection.

Yarn
Cascade Yarns Cherub Bulky; super bulky weight #6; 55% nylon/45% acrylic; 7.05 oz (200 g)/ 131 yd (120 m) per skein
- 1 skein each: 01 White (**A**), 87 Dahlia Purple (**B**), 82 Desert Flower (**C**)

Hook and Other Materials
- US size J-10 (6 mm) crochet hook
- Yarn needle
- Poly-fil stuffing
- Two 15 mm safety eyes
- Stitch markers

Finished Measurement
About 16 in (40.5 cm) tall

Gauge
11 sc and 11 rows/rounds = 4 in (10 cm)

Special Stitch
Invisible single crochet 2 together (sc2tog): Insert hook in the FLO of next 2 sts, yarn over and draw through both sts, yarn over and draw through 2 loops on hook (1 stitch decreased).

Pattern Note
Butterfly is made in 11 pieces: Head, Body, 4 Wings, 2 Antennae, 2 Spots, and a Flower.

INSTRUCTIONS

Head
Rnd 1 (RS): With **A**, create magic ring, 7 sc in ring; do not join. (7 sc) Place marker to indicate beginning of rnd.
Note: Loop a short piece of yarn around any stitch to mark Rnd 1 as right side. Move stitch marker up with each rnd.
Rnd 2: 2 sc in each st around. (14 sc)
Rnd 3: (Sc in next st, 2 sc in next st) around. (21 sc)
Rnd 4: (Sc in next 2 sts, 2 sc in next st) around. (28 sc)
Rnd 5: (Sc in next 3 sts, 2 sc in next st) around. (35 sc)

Rnd 6: (Sc in next 4 sts, 2 sc in next st) around. (42 sc)
Rnd 7: (Sc in next 5 sts, 2 sc in next st) around. (49 sc)
Rnd 8: (Sc in next 6 sts, 2 sc in next st) around. (56 sc)
Rnd 9: (Sc in next 7 sts, 2 sc in next st) around. (63 sc)
Rnd 10: Sc in each st around.
Rnd 11: (Sc in next 8 sts, 2 sc in next st) around. (70 sc)
Rnds 12–20: Sc in each st around.
Add safety eyes between Rnds 14 and 15 about 6 sts apart.
Rnd 21: (Sc in next 8 sts, sc2tog) around. (63 sc)

Rnd 22: Sc in each st around.
Rnd 23: (Sc in next 7 sts, sc2tog) around. (56 sc)
Rnd 24: (Sc in next 6 sts, sc2tog) around. (49 sc)
Rnd 25: (Sc in next 5 sts, sc2tog) around. (42 sc)
Rnd 26: (Sc in next 4 sts, sc2tog) around. (35 sc)
Rnd 27: (Sc in next 3 sts, sc2tog) around. (28 sc)
Rnd 28: (Sc in next 2 sts, sc2tog) around. (21 sc)
Fasten off.
Stuff Head firmly.

Body
Rnd 29: Join **B**, 2 sc in each st around. (42 sc)
Rnd 30: (Sc in next 5 sts, 2 sc in next st) around.
    (49 sc)
Rnd 31: Sc in each st around.
Rnd 32: (Sc in next 6 sts, 2sc in next st) around.
    (56 sc)
Rnds 33–49: Sc in each st around.
Rnd 50: (Sc in next 6 sts, sc2tog) around. (49 sc)
Drop **B**, join **C**.
Rnd 51: Sc in each st around.
Drop **C**, pick up **B**.
Rnd 52: (Sc in next 5 sts, sc2tog) around. (42 sc)
Drop **B**, pick up **C**.
Rnd 53: Sc in each st around.
Drop **C**, pick up **B**.

Rnd 54: (Sc in next 4 sts, sc2tog) around. (35 sc)
Drop **B**, pick up **C**.
Rnd 55: Sc in each st around.
Drop **C**, pick up **B**.
Rnd 56: (Sc in next 3 sts, sc2tog) around. (28 sc)
Fasten off **B**, pick up **C**.
Rnd 57: Sc in each st around.
Stuff Body.
Rnd 58: (Sc in next 2 sts, sc2tog) around. (21 sc)
Rnd 59: Sc in each st around.
Rnd 60: (Sc in next st, sc2tog) around. (14 sc)
Rnd 61: Sc in each st around.
Stuff firmly.
Rnd 62: (Sc2tog) 7 times. (7 sc)
Fasten off, leaving a long tail for sewing.
Use yarn needle and long tail to close Rnd 62.

Top Wing (make 2)
Rnd 1 (RS): With **C**, create magic ring, 6 sc in ring;
    do not join. (6 sc) Place marker to indicate begin-
    ning of rnd.
Note: Loop a short piece of yarn around any stitch
    to mark Rnd 1 as right side. Move stitch marker
    up with each rnd.
Rnd 2: 2 sc in each st around. (12 sc)
Rnd 3: (Sc in next st, 2 sc in next st) around. (18 sc)
Rnd 4: (Sc in next 2 sts, 2 sc in next st) around.
    (24 sc)
Rnd 5: (Sc in next 3 sts, 2 sc in next st) around.
    (30 sc)
Rnd 6: (Sc in next 4 sts, 2 sc in next st) around.
    (36 sc)
Rnds 7–13: Sc in each st around.
Rnd 14: (Sc in next 4 sts, sc2tog) around. (30 sc)
Rnd 15: (Sc in next 13 sts, sc2tog) around. (28 sc)
Rnd 16: (Sc in next 12 sts, sc2tog) around. (26 sc)
Rnd 17: (Sc in next 11 sts, sc2tog) around. (24 sc)
Rnd 18: (Sc in next 4 sts, sc2tog) around. (20 sc)
Rnd 19: (Sc in next 3 sts, sc2tog) around. (16 sc)
Rnd 20: (Sc in next 2 sts, sc2tog) around. (12 sc)
Fasten off, leaving a long tail for sewing.

Base Wing (make 2)
Rnd 1 (RS): With **A**, create magic ring, 6 sc in ring;
    do not join. (6 sc) Place marker to indicate begin-
    ning of rnd.
Note: Loop a short piece of yarn around any stitch
    to mark Rnd 1 as right side. Move stitch marker
    up with each rnd.
Rnd 2: 2 sc in each st around. (12 sc)
Rnd 3: (Sc in next st, 2 sc in next st) around. (18 sc)

Rnd 4: (Sc in next 2 sts, 2 sc in next st) around. (24 sc)

Rnd 5: (Sc in next 3 sts, 2 sc in next st) around. (30 sc)

Rnds 6–14: Sc in each st around.

Rnd 15: (Sc in next 13 sts, sc2tog) around. (28 sc)

Rnd 16: (Sc in next 12 sts, sc2tog) around. (26 sc)

Rnd 17: (Sc in next 11 sts, sc2tog) around. (24 sc)

Rnd 18: (Sc in next 4 sts, sc2tog) around. (20 sc)

Rnd 19: (Sc in next 3 sts, sc2tog) around. (16 sc)

Rnd 20: (Sc in next 2 sts, sc2tog) around. (12 sc)

Fasten off, leaving a long tail for sewing.

Wing Spot (make 2)

Rnd 1 (RS): With **B**, create magic ring, 6 sc in ring; do not join. (6 sc) Place marker to indicate beginning of rnd.

Note: Loop a short piece of yarn around any stitch to mark Rnd 1 as right side. Move stitch marker up with each rnd.

Rnd 2: 2 sc in each st around. (12 sc)

Fasten off, leaving a long tail for sewing.

Antenna (make 2)

Using photo as a guide, join **B** using stitch post above safety eyes, ch 5. Fasten off. Trim. Repeat above other eye.

Flower

Rnd 1 (RS): With **C**, create magic ring, 5 sc in ring; do not join. (5 sc)

Rnd 2: (Sl st, ch 1, dc, ch 1, sl st) in each st around (5 petals)

Fasten off, leaving a long tail for sewing.

Assembly

Use photos as a guide.

Sew Wings on Body toward outer edge so they are shown in full in front of Body. Stitch to Body as needed to hold in place.

Sew Wing Spots on Top Wings.

With **C**, stitch a decor line on chest on Body.

Sew Flower on side of one Antenna.

Gruff the Dragon

This baby dragon brings the spunk to this supersize collection! I'm not sure his wings will lift that chunky body, but he will waddle to join in any playtime session.

Yarn
Cascade Yarns Cherub Bulky; super bulky weight
    #6; 55% nylon/45% acrylic; 7.05 oz (200 g)/
    131 yd (120 m) per skein
- 3 skeins: 30 Papaya (**A**)
- 1 skein each: 38 Yellow (**B**), 11 Lime (**C**)

Hook and Other Materials
- US size J-10 (6 mm) crochet hook
- Yarn needle
- Poly-fil stuffing
- Two 15 mm safety eyes
- Stitch markers

Finished Measurements
About 14 in (35.5 cm) tall

Gauge
11 sc and 11 rows/rounds = 4 in (10 cm)

Special Stitches
Invisible single crochet 2 together (sc2tog): Insert
    hook in the FLO of next 2 sts, yarn over and draw
    through both sts, yarn over and draw through 2
    loops on hook (1 stitch decreased).
Picot: Ch 3, sl st to first ch.

Pattern Note
Dragon is made in 15 pieces: Body, 3 Horns, 2 Ears,
    Belly, Snout, Tail, 2 Arms, 2 Feet, and 2 Wings.

INSTRUCTIONS

Body

Rnd 1 (RS): With **A**, create magic ring, 8 sc in ring; do not join. (8 sc) Place marker to indicate beginning of rnd.

Note: Loop a short piece of yarn around any stitch to mark Rnd 1 as right side. Move stitch marker up with each rnd.

Rnd 2: 2 sc in each st around. (16 sc)

Rnd 3: (Sc in next st, 2 sc in next st) around. (24 sc)

Rnd 4: (Sc in next 2 sts, 2 sc in next st) around. (32 sc)

Rnd 5: Sc in each st around.

Rnd 6: (Sc in next 3 sts, 2 sc in next st) around. (40 sc)

Rnd 7: (Sc in next 4 sts, 2 sc in next st) around. (48 sc)

Rnds 8–11: Sc in each st around.

Rnd 12: (Sc in next 5 sts, 2 sc in next st) around. (56 sc)

Rnd 13: Sc in each st around.

Rnd 14: (Sc in next 6 sts, 2 sc in next st) around. (64 sc)

Rnds 15–41: Sc in each st around.

Add safety eyes between Rnds 13 and 14 about 6 sts apart.

Rnd 42: (Sc in next 6 sts, sc2tog) around. (56 sc)

Rnd 43: Sc in each st around.

Rnd 44: (Sc in next 5 sts, sc2tog) around. (48 sc)

Rnd 45: Sc in each st around.

Rnd 46: (Sc in next 4 sts, sc2tog) around. (40 sc)

Rnd 47: (Sc in next 3 sts, sc2tog) around. (32 sc)

Stuff Body firmly.

Rnd 48: (Sc in next 2 sts, sc2tog) around. (24 sc)

Rnd 49: (Sc in next st, sc2tog) around. (16 sc)

Rnd 50: (Sc2tog) 8 times. (8 sc)

Fasten off, leaving a long tail for sewing.

Use yarn needle and long tail to close Rnd 50.

Belly

With **B**, ch 6.

Row 1 (WS): 2 sc in 2nd ch from hook, sc in next 3 sts, 2 sc in last st, turn. (7 sc)

Row 2 (RS): Ch 1, 2 sc in first st, sc in next 5 sts, 2 sc in next st, turn. (9 sc)

Row 3: Ch 1, sc in each st across, turn.

Row 4: Ch 1, 2 sc in first st, sc in next 7 sts, 2 sc in next st, turn. (11 sc)

Row 5: Ch 1, 2 sc in first st, sc in next 9 sts, 2 sc in next st, turn. (13 sc)

Row 6: Ch 1, sc in each st across, turn.

Row 7: Ch 1, 2 sc in first st, sc in next 11 sts, 2 sc in next st, turn. (15 sc)

Rows 8–13: Ch 1, sc in each st across, turn.

Row 14: Ch 1, sc2tog, sc in next 11 sts, sc2tog, turn. (13 sc)

Row 15: Ch 1, sc in each st across, turn.

Row 16: Ch 1, sc2tog, sc in next 9 sts, sc2tog, turn. (11 sc)

Row 17: Ch 1, st in each st across, turn.

Border

Rnd 1 (RS): Ch 1, (sc2tog) 2 times, sc in next 7 sts, (sc2tog) 2 times, sc 17 evenly down ends of rows, sc 5 across Row 1, sc 17 evenly down ends of rows; join with sl st to first sc.

Fasten off, leaving a long tail for sewing.

Tail

Rnd 1 (RS): With **A**, create magic ring, 4 sc in ring; do not join. (4 sc) Place marker to indicate beginning of rnd.

Note: Loop a short piece of yarn around any stitch to mark Rnd 1 as right side. Move stitch marker up with each rnd.

Rnd 2: 2 sc in next st, sc in next 3 sts. (5 sc)

Rnd 3: 2 sc in next st, sc in next 4 sts. (6 sc)

Rnd 4: 2 sc in next st, sc in next 5 sts. (7 sc)

Rnd 5: 2 sc in next st, sc in next 6 sts. (8 sc)

Rnd 6: 2 sc in next st, sc in next 7 sts. (9 sc)

Rnd 7: 2 sc in next st, sc in next 8 sts. (10 sc)

Rnd 8: 2 sc in next st, sc in next 9 sts. (11 sc)

Rnd 9: 2 sc in next st, sc in next 10 sts. (12 sc)

Rnd 10: 2 sc in next st, sc in next 11 sts. (13 sc)

Rnd 11: 2 sc in next st, sc in next 12 sts. (14 sc)

Rnd 12: 2 sc in next st, sc in next 13 sts. (15 sc)

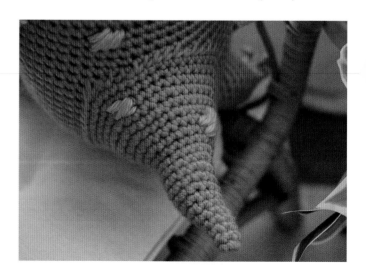

Rnd 13: 2 sc in next st, sc in next 14 sts. (16 sc)

Rnd 14: (2 sc in next st, sc in next 7 sts) around. (18 sc)

Rnd 15: (Sc in next 2 sts, 2 sc in next st) around. (24 sc)

Rnd 16: Sc in each st around.

Rnd 17: (Sc in next 3 sts, 2 sc in next st) around. (30 sc)

Rnd 18: Sc in each st around.

Rnd 19: (Sc in next 4 sts, 2 sc in next st) around. (36 sc)

Rnd 20: Sc in each st around.

Rnd 21: (Sc in next 5 sts, 2 sc in next st) around. (42 sc)

Rnd 22: (Sc in next 6 sts, 2 sc in next st) around. (48 sc)

Fasten off, leaving a long tail for sewing.

Snout

With **A**, ch 6.

Rnd 1 (RS): 2 sc in 2nd ch from hook, sc in next 3 ch, 4 sc in last ch, working on opposite side of ch, sc in next 3 chs, 2 sc in last ch; join with sl st to first sc. (14 sc)

Rnd 2: Ch 1, 2 sc in next 2 sts, sc in next 3 sts, 2 sc in next 4 sts, sc in next 3 sts, 2 sc in next 2 sts; join with sl st to first sc. (22 sc)

Rnds 3–5: Ch 1, sc in each st around; join with sl st to first sc.

Fasten off, leaving a long tail for sewing.

Ear (make 2)

With **A**, ch 2.

Row 1 (RS): 6 sc in 2nd ch from hook, turn. (6 sc)

Row 2: Ch 3 (counts as dc), dc in same st, 2 dc in each st across. (12 dc)

Fasten off, leaving a long tail for sewing.

Fold open ends and sew together.

Horn (make 3)

Rnd 1 (RS): With **B**, create magic ring, 4 sc in ring; do not join. (4 sc) Place marker to indicate beginning of rnd.

Note: Loop a short piece of yarn around any stitch to mark Rnd 1 as right side. Move stitch marker up with each rnd.

Rnd 2: 2 sc in next st, sc in next 3 sts. (5 sc)

Rnd 3: 2 sc in next st, sc in next 4 sts. (6 sc)

Rnd 4: 2 sc in next st, sc in next 5 sts. (7 sc)

Rnd 5: 2 sc in next st, sc in next 6 sts. (8 sc)

Fasten off, leaving a long tail for sewing.

Wing (make 2)

Rnd 1 (RS): With **B**, ch 4, 9 dc in 4th ch from hook; join with sl st to beg ch-4. (10 dc) Place marker to indicate beginning of rnd.

Note: Loop a short piece of yarn around any stitch to mark Rnd 1 as right side. Move stitch marker up with each rnd.

Rnd 2: Ch 2 (not a st), 2 dc in each st around; join with sl st to first dc. (20 dc)

Rnd 3: Ch 2, (dc in next st, 2 dc in next st) around; join with sl st to first dc. (30 dc)

Rnd 4: Ch 2, (dc in next 2 sts, 2 dc in next st) around; join with sl st to first dc. (40 dc)

Fold circle in half with first stitch lining up with last st; work through both sides as ONE stitch for a total of 20 sts across. This will close the circle and add an edge detail.

Row 1: Ch 1, working through 2 sts as one (front and back of folded circle), (sc, ch 3, sc) in first st, sc in next 2 sts, *(sc, ch 3, sc) in next st, sc in next 3 sts; rep from * across to last 4 sts, (sc, ch 3, sc) in next st, sc in next 2 sts, (sc, ch 3, sc) in last st.

Fasten off.

Arm (make 2)

With **A**, ch 8; join with sl st to first ch to form ring.

Rnd 1 (RS): Ch 1, 8 sc in ring; do not join. (8 sc) Place marker to indicate beginning of rnd.

Note: Loop a short piece of yarn around any stitch to mark Rnd 1 as right side. Move stitch marker up with each rnd.

Rnd 2: (Sc in next st, 2 sc in next st) around. (12 sc)

Rnds 3–5: Sc in each st around.

Rnd 6: (Sc in next st, sc2tog). (8 sc)

Fasten off, leaving a long tail for sewing.

Thread needle with **A** and sew Rnd 1 flat.

Do not stuff.

Foot (make 2)

With **A**, ch 16; join with sl st to first ch to form ring.

Rnd 1 (RS): Ch 1, 16 sc in ring; do not join. (16 sc) Place marker to indicate beginning of rnd.

Note: Loop a short piece of yarn around any stitch to mark Rnd 1 as right side. Move stitch marker up with each rnd.

Rnd 2: Sc in each st around.

Rnd 3: (Sc in next 3 sts, 2 sc in next st) around. (20 sc)

Rnd 4: Sc in each st around.

Rnd 5: (Sc in next 4 sts, 2 sc in next st) around. (24 sc)

Rnd 6: Sc in each st around.

Rnds 7–9: Sc in each st around.

Rnd 10: (Sc in next 4 sts, sc2tog) around. (20 sc)

Rnd 11: (Sc in next 3 sts, sc2tog) around. (16 sc)

Rnd 12: (Sc in next 2 sts, sc2tog) around. (12 sc)

Stuff end of Foot lightly before closing.

Fold circle in half with first stitch lining up with last st; work through both sides as ONE stitch for a total of 6 sts across. This will close the circle and add an edge detail.

Row 1: Ch 1, working through 2 sts as one (front and back of folded circle), *ch 2, dc in next st, picot, ch 2, sl st in next st; rep from * across.

Fasten off, leaving a long tail for sewing.

Assembly

Use photos as a guide.

Sew Horns, Ears, and Snout on head.

Sew Wings on back of Body.

Sew Belly on Body.

Sew Arms on each side of Body.

Sew Feet on base of Body.

Finishing

Use yarn needle and **C** and stitch on spots on Body.

Tucky the Turtle

Tucky might be slow to the party, but he'll snap into action when yarn is involved! He is a quick project to crochet with a 10-star cuteness factor!

Yarn

Yarnspirations Bernat Softee Chunky; super bulky weight #6; 100% acrylic; 3.5 oz (100 g)/108 yd (99 m) per skein
- 3 skeins: 28031 Linen (**A**)

Berroco Yarns Coco; super bulky weight #6; 100% superwash merino wool; 3.5 oz (100 g)/77 yd (70 m) per skein

3 skeins: 4915 Pampas (**B**)

Hooks and Other Materials

- US size J-10 (6 mm) crochet hook
- US size I (6.5 mm) crochet hook
- Yarn needle
- Poly-fil stuffing
- Two 15 mm safety eyes
- Stitch markers

Finished Measurements

Head to back of shell: about 17 in (43 cm)
About 8¼ in (21 cm) high

Gauge

With smaller hook and **A**, 11 sc and 11 rows/rounds = 4 in (10 cm)

Special Stitch

Invisible single crochet 2 together (sc2tog): Insert hook in the FLO of next 2 sts, yarn over and draw through both sts, yarn over and draw through 2 loops on hook (1 stitch decreased).

Pattern Note

Turtle is made in 7 pieces: Head, Shell Top, Shell Base, and 4 Feet.

INSTRUCTIONS

Head

Rnd 1 (RS): With **A** and smaller hook, create magic ring, 6 sc in ring; do not join. (6 sc) Place marker to indicate beginning of rnd.

Note: Loop a short piece of yarn around any stitch to mark Rnd 1 as right side. Move stitch marker up with each rnd.

Rnd 2: 2 sc in each st around. (12 sc)

Rnd 3: (Sc in next st, 2 sc in next st) around. (18 sc)

Rnd 4: (Sc in next 2 sts, 2 sc in next st) around. (24 sc)

Rnd 5: (Sc in next 3 sts, 2 sc in next st) around. (30 sc)

Rnd 6: (Sc in next 4 sts, 2 sc in next st) around. (36 sc)

Rnd 7: (Sc in next 5 sts, 2 sc in next st) around. (42 sc)

Rnd 8: (Sc in next 6 sts, 2 sc in next st) around. (48 sc)

Rnds 9–14: Sc in each st around.

Add safety eyes between Rnds 10 and 11 about 4 sts apart.

Rnd 15: (Sc in next 6 sts, sc2tog) around. (42 sc)

Rnd 16: (Sc in next 5 sts, sc2tog) around. (36 sc)

Rnd 17: (Sc in next 4 sts, sc2tog) around. (30 sc)

Rnd 18: (Sc in next 3 sts, sc2tog) around. (24 sc)

Rnd 19: (Sc in next 2 sts, sc2tog) around. (18 sc)

Stuff Head firmly.

Rnds 20–29: Sc in each st around.

Lightly stuff neck.

Fasten off, leaving a long tail for sewing.

Shell Top

Rnd 1 (RS): With **B** and larger hook, create magic ring, 7 sc in ring; do not join. (7 sc) Place marker to indicate beginning of rnd.

Note: Loop a short piece of yarn around any stitch to mark Rnd 1 as right side. Move stitch marker up with each rnd.

Rnd 2: 2 sc in each st around. (14 sc)

Rnd 3: (Sc in next st, 2 sc in next st) around. (21 sc)

Rnd 4: (Sc in next 2 sts, 2 sc in next st) around. (28 sc)

Rnd 5: (Sc in next 3 sts, 2 sc in next st) around. (35 sc)

Rnd 6: (Sc in next 4 sts, 2 sc in next st) around. (42 sc)

Rnd 7: (Sc in next 5 sts, 2 sc in next st) around. (49 sc)

Rnd 8: (Sc in next 6 sts, 2 sc in next st) around. (56 sc)

Rnd 9: (Sc in next 7 sts, 2 sc in next st) around. (63 sc)

Rnd 10: (Sc in next 8 sts, 2 sc in next st) around. (70 sc)

Rnd 11: Sc in each st around.

Rnd 12: (Sc in next 9 sts, 2 sc in next st) around. (77 sc)

Rnd 13: (Sc in next 10 sts, 2 sc in next st) around. (84 sc)

Rnd 14: (Sc in next 11 sts, 2 sc in next st) around. (91 sc)

Rnd 15: (Sc in next 12 sts, 2 sc in next st) around. (98 sc)

Rnds 16–27: Sc in each st around.

Rnd 28: (Sc in next 12 sts, sc2tog) around. (91 sc)

Rnd 29: Sc in each st around.

Rnd 30: (Sc in next 11 sts, sc2tog) around. (84 sc)

Rnd 31: Sc in each st around.

Rnd 32: (Sc in next 10 sts, sc2tog) around. (77 sc)

Rnd 33: Sc in each st around.

Fasten off.

Shell Base

Rnd 1 (RS): With **A** and smaller hook, create magic ring, 7 sc in ring; do not join. (7 sc) Place marker to indicate beginning of rnd.

Note: Loop a short piece of yarn around any stitch to mark Rnd 1 as right side. Move stitch marker up with each rnd.

Rnd 2: 2 sc in each st around. (14 sc)

Rnd 3: (Sc in next st, 2 sc in next st) around. (21 sc)

Rnd 4: (Sc in next 2 sts, 2 sc in next st) around. (28 sc)

Rnd 5: (Sc in next 3 sts, 2 sc in next st) around. (35 sc)

Rnd 6: (Sc in next 4 sts, 2 sc in next st) around. (42 sc)

Rnd 7: (Sc in next 5 sts, 2 sc in next st) around. (49 sc)

Rnd 8: (Sc in next 6 sts, 2 sc in next st) around. (56 sc)

Rnd 9: (Sc in next 7 sts, 2 sc in next st) around. (63 sc)

Rnd 10: (Sc in next 8 sts, 2 sc in next st) around. (70 sc)

Rnd 11: Sc in each st around.

Rnd 12: (Sc in next 9 sts, 2 sc in next st) around. (77 sc)

Fasten off.

Shell Assembly

Rnd 1: With **A** and smaller hook, ch 1, sl st through Shell Top and Shell Base, stuffing before closing.

Foot (make 4)

Rnd 1 (RS): With **A**, create magic ring, 6 sc in ring; do not join. (6 sc) Place marker to indicate beginning of rnd.

Note: Loop a short piece of yarn around any stitch to mark Rnd 1 as right side. Move stitch marker up with each rnd.

Rnd 2: 2 sc in each st around. (12 sc)

Rnd 3: (Sc in next st, 2 sc in next st) around. (18 sc)

Rnd 4: (Sc in next 2 sts, 2 sc in next st) around. (24 sc)

Rnd 5: (Sc in next 3 sts, 2 sc in next st) around. (30 sc)

Rnd 6: (Sc in next 4 sts, 2 sc in next st) around. (36 sc)

Rnd 7: (Sc in next 5 sts, 2 sc in next st) around. (42 sc)

Rnd 8: (Sc in next 6 sts, 2 sc in next st) around. (48 sc)

Rnd 9: (Sc in next 7 sts, 2 sc in next st) around. (54 sc)

Fasten off, leaving a long tail for sewing.

Fold circle in half and sew closed.

Assembly
Use photos as a guide.
Sew neck opening on Shell at joining seam.
Stitch the back of Head on Shell to fix Head in
    place.
Sew Feet on Shell Base.

Ryno-Dino

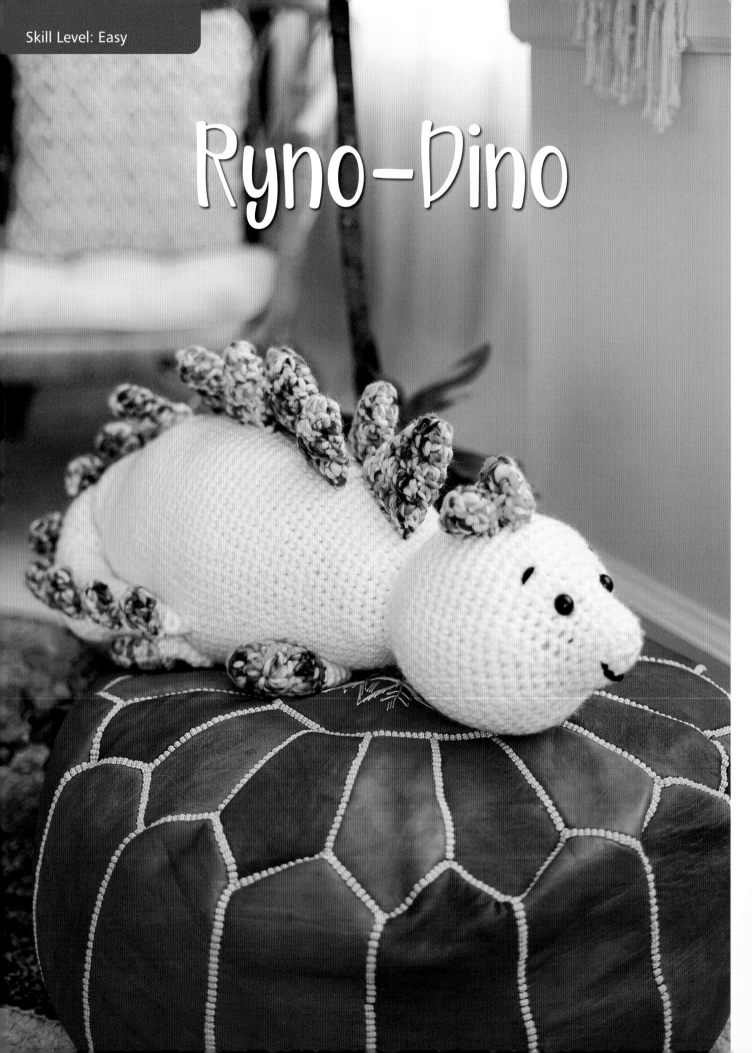

Don't let Ryno-Dino's spikes fool you—he loves to snuggle! Curl up with this dinosaur for a midday nap or book time! He is worked in a solid color from the tip of his tail to the tip of his nose, with a fun contrasting variegated yarn for the spikes. Have fun mixing your colors!

Yarn
Cascade Yarns Cherub Bulky; super bulky weight #6; 55% nylon/45% acrylic; 7.05 oz (200 g)/ 131 yd (120 m) per skein
- 2 skeins: 01 White (**A**)
- 1 skein: 40 Black (**B**) (eyebrow and mouth detail only)

Berroco Yarns Coco; super bulky weight #6; 100% superwash merino wool; 3.5 oz (100 g)/77 yd (70 m) per skein
- 3 skeins: 4929 Pool (**C**)

Hooks and Other Materials
- US size J-10 (6 mm) crochet hook
- US size I (6.5 mm) crochet hook
- Yarn needle
- Poly-fil stuffing
- Two 15 mm safety eyes
- Stitch markers

Finished Measurement
About 23 in (58.5 cm) long

Gauge
With **A** and smaller hook, 11 sc and 11 rows/rounds = 4 in (10 cm)

Special Stitch
Invisible single crochet 2 together (sc2tog): Insert hook in the FLO of next 2 sts, yarn over and draw through both sts, yarn over and draw through 2 loops on hook (1 stitch decreased).

Pattern Note
Dino is made in 25 pieces: Tail, Body, Head, 4 Legs, 10 Small Spikes, 5 Medium Spikes, and 3 Large Spikes.

INSTRUCTIONS

Tail
Rnd 1 (RS): With **A** and smaller hook, create magic ring, 6 sc in ring; do not join. (6 sc) Place marker to indicate beginning of rnd.

Note: Loop a short piece of yarn around any stitch to mark Rnd 1 as right side. Move stitch marker up with each rnd.

Rnd 2: 2 sc in next st, sc in next 5 sts. (7 sc)
Rnd 3: Sc in each st around.
Rnd 4: 2 sc in next st, sc in next 6 sts. (8 sc)
Rnd 5: 2 sc in next st, sc in next 7 sts. (9 sc)
Rnd 6: 2 sc in next st, sc in next 8 sts. (10 sc)
Rnd 7: 2 sc in next st, sc in next 9 sts. (11 sc)
Rnd 8: 2 sc in next st, sc in next 10 sts. (12 sc)
Rnd 9: 2 sc in next st, sc in next 11 sts. (13 sc)
Rnd 10: 2 sc in next st, sc in next 12 sts. (14 sc)
Rnd 11: 2 sc in next st, sc in next 13 sts. (15 sc)

Rnd 12: 2 sc in next st, sc in next 14 sts. (16 sc)
Rnd 13: 2 sc in next st, sc in next 15 sts. (17 sc)
Rnd 14: 2 sc in next st, sc in next 16 sts. (18 sc)
Rnd 15: 2 sc in next st, sc in next 17 sts. (19 sc)
Rnd 16: 2 sc in next st, sc in next 18 sts. (20 sc)
Rnd 17: 2 sc in next st, sc in next 19 sts. (21 sc)
Rnd 18: 2 sc in next st, sc in next 20 sts. (22 sc)
Rnd 19: 2 sc in next st, sc in next 21 sts. (23 sc)
Rnd 20: 2 sc in next st, sc in next 22 sts. (24 sc)
Rnd 21: 2 sc in next st, sc in next 23 sts. (25 sc)
Rnd 22: 2 sc in next st, sc in next 24 sts. (26 sc)
Rnd 23: 2 sc in next st, sc in next 25 sts. (27 sc)
Rnd 24: 2 sc in next st, sc in next 26 sts. (28 sc)
Rnd 25: 2 sc in next st, sc in next 27 sts. (29 sc)
Rnd 26: 2 sc in next st, sc in next 28 sts. (30 sc)
Rnd 27: 2 sc in next st, sc in next 29 sts. (31 sc)
Rnd 28: 2 sc in next st, sc in next 30 sts. (32 sc)
Rnd 29: 2 sc in next st, sc in next 31 sts. (33 sc)
Rnd 30: 2 sc in next st, sc in next 32 sts. (34 sc)
Rnd 31: 2 sc in next st, sc in next 33 sts. (35 sc)
Rnd 32: 2 sc in next st, sc in next 34 sts. (36 sc)
Rnd 33: 2 sc in next st, sc in next 35 sts. (37 sc)
Rnd 34: 2 sc in next st, sc in next 36 sts. (38 sc)
Rnd 35: 2 sc in next st, sc in next 37 sts. (39 sc)
Rnd 36: 2 sc in next st, sc in next 38 sts. (40 sc)
Rnd 37: 2 sc in next st, sc in next 39 sts. (41 sc)
Rnd 38: 2 sc in next st, sc in next 40 sts. (42 sc)
Stuff Tail firmly.

Body

Rnd 39: (Sc in next 6 sts, 2 sc in next st) around. (48 sc)
Rnds 40–41: Sc in each st around.
Rnd 42: (Sc in next 7 sts, 2 sc in next st) around. (54 sc)
Rnds 43–44: Sc in each st around.
Rnd 45: (Sc in next 8 sts, 2 sc in next st) around. (60 sc)
Rnds 46–47: Sc in each st around.
Rnd 48: (Sc in next 14 sts, 2 sc in next st) around. (64 sc)
Rnds 49–60: Sc in each st around.
Note: Mark Rnd 55 with a stitch marker.
Rnd 61: (Sc in next 14 sts, sc2tog) around. (60 sc)
Rnd 62: Sc in each st around.
Rnd 63: (Sc in next 8 sts, sc2tog) around. (54 sc)
Rnds 64–66: Sc in each st around.
Rnd 67: (Sc in next 7 sts, sc2tog) around. (48 sc)
Rnds 68–70: Sc in each st around.
Rnd 71: (Sc in next 6 sts, sctog) around. (42 sc)
Rnds 72–73: Sc in each st around.

Rnd 74: (Sc in next 5 sts, sc2tog) around. (36 sc)
Rnds 75–76: Sc in each st around.
Rnd 77: (Sc in next 4 sts, sc2tog) around. (30 sc)
Rnd 78: Sc in each st around.
Rnd 79: (Sc in next 3 sts, sc2tog) around. (24 sc)
Stuff Body firmly.

Head

Rnd 80: (Sc in next 2 sts, 2 sc in next st) around. (32 sc)
Rnd 81: (Sc in next 3 sts, 2 sc in next st) around. (40 sc)
Rnd 82: (Sc in next 4 sts, 2 sc in next st) around. (48 sc)
Rnds 83–92: Sc in each st around.
Rnd 93: (Sc in next 4 sts, sc2tog) around. (40 sc)
Rnd 94: (Sc in next 3 sts, sc2tog) around. (32 sc)
Rnd 95: (Sc in next 2 sts, sc2tog) around. (24 sc)
Rnd 96: (Sc in next st, sc2tog) around. (16 sc)
Stuff Head firmly.
Add safety eyes between Rnds 95 and 96 about 5 sts apart.
Rnds 97–100: Sc in each st around.
Rnd 101: (Sc2tog) 8 times. (8 sc)
Fasten off, leaving a long tail for sewing.
Thread needle with long tail and close Rnd 101.

Leg (make 4)

With **B** and larger hook, ch 4.

Rnd 1 (RS): 9 dc in 4th ch from hook; join with sl st to beg ch-4. (10 dc)

Rnd 2: Ch 3 (counts as dc), dc in same st as joining, 2 dc in each st around; join with sl st to beg ch-3. (20 dc)

Fasten off.

Rnd 3: Join **A** with smaller hook in any st, ch 1, working in the BLO, sc in each st around; join with sl st to first sc.

Rnd 4: Ch 1, sc in each st around; do not join.

Rnds 5–7: Sc in each st around.

Fasten off, leaving a long tail for sewing.

Stuff lightly.

Small Spike (make 10: 3 for head and 7 for tail/body)

With **B** and larger hook, ch 4.

Rnd 1: 5 dc in 4th ch from hook; join with sl st to beg ch-4. (6 dc)

Rnd 2: Ch 3 (counts as dc), dc in same st, dc in next 2 sts, 2 dc in next st, dc in next 2 sts; join with sl st to beg ch-3. (8 dc)

Fasten off, leaving a long tail for sewing.

Medium Spike (make 5)

With **B** and larger hook, ch 4.

Rnd 1: 5 dc in 4th ch from hook; join with sl st to beg ch-4. (6 dc)

Rnd 2: Ch 3 (counts as dc), dc in same st, dc in next 2 sts, 2 dc in next st, dc in next 2 sts; join with sl st to beg ch-3. (8 dc)

Rnd 3: Ch 3 (counts as dc), dc in same st, dc in next 3 sts, 2 dc in next st, dc in next 3 sts; join with sl st to beg ch-3. (10 dc)

Rnd 4: Ch 3 (counts as dc), dc in same st, dc in next 4 sts, 2 dc in next st, dc in next 4 sts; join with sl st to beg ch-3. (12 dc)

Fasten off, leaving a long tail for sewing.

Large Spike (make 3)

With **B** and larger hook, ch 4.

Rnd 1: 5 dc in 4th ch from hook; join with sl st to beg ch-4. (6 dc)

Rnd 2: Ch 3 (counts as dc), dc in same st, dc in next dc, (2 dc in next dc, dc in next dc) around; join with sl st to beg ch-3. (9 dc)

Rnd 3: Ch 3 (counts as dc), dc in same st, dc in next 2 dc, (2 dc in next dc, dc in next 2 dc) around; join with sl st to beg ch-3. (12 dc)

Rnd 4: Ch 3 (counts as dc), dc in same st, dc in next 3 dc, (2 dc in next dc, dc in next 3 dc) around; join with sl st to beg ch-3. (15 dc)

Rnd 5: Ch 3 (counts as dc), dc in same st, dc in next 4 dc, (2 dc in next dc, dc in next 4 dc) around; join with sl st to beg ch-3. (18 dc)

Fasten off, leaving a long tail for sewing.

Assembly

Use photos as a guide.

Pull tip of Tail to Body on marked Rnd 55 and stitch together to secure at tip and along body with yarn needle and **A**.

Sew 7 Small Spikes evenly from tip of Tail to Body.

Then sew 1 Medium Spike, 3 Large Spikes in order.

On outside of Large Spikes, sew 2 Medium Spikes closely on each side.

Sew 3 Small Spikes across the top of Head.

Sew Legs on Body.

Larry the Llama

Llamas are my favorite. They have such a supersize personality! This llama wants to play—but no spitting! Enjoy this fluffy pattern and your playtime with your new amigurumi.

Yarn

Lion Brand Yarns Go For Faux Thick & Quick; jumbo weight #7; 100% polyester; 4.2 oz (120 g)/ 24 yd (22 m) per skein
• 8 skeins: 323-098 Baked Alaska (**A**)

Cascade Yarns Cherub Bulky; super bulky weight #6; 55% nylon/45% acrylic; 7.05 oz (200 g)/ 131 yd (120 m) per skein
• 2 skeins: 01 White (**B**)

Cascade Yarns Pacific Bulky; super bulky weight #6; 60% acrylic/40% superwash merino wool; 7.05 oz (200 g)/129 yd (118 m) per skein
• 1 skein each: 30 Latte (**C**), 33 Cactus (**D**), 115 Golden (**E**)

Hooks and Other Materials

• US size J-10 (6 mm) crochet hook
• US size N-13 (9 mm) crochet hook
• Yarn needle
• Poly-fil stuffing
• Two 15 mm safety eyes
• Stitch markers

Finished Measurements

About 9 in (23 cm) to top of body and 16 in (40.5 cm) to top of head
About 13 in (33 cm) wide

Gauge

With **A** and smaller hook, 11 sc and 11 rows/rounds = 4 in (10 cm)

Special Stitch

Invisible single crochet 2 together (sc2tog): Insert hook in the FLO of next 2 sts, yarn over and draw through both sts, yarn over and draw through 2 loops on hook (1 stitch decreased).

Pattern Notes

- Llama is made in 10 pieces: Body, Neck, Head, 2 Ears, 4 Feet, and Blanket.
- This amigurumi is primarily made with a jumbo #7 yarn, but crocheting a mini with medium-weight #4 yarn will not convert to similar proportions.

INSTRUCTIONS

Body

Beg at back end of body, with larger hook and **A**, ch 2.

Rnd 1 (RS): With **A**, create magic ring, 8 sc in ring; do not join. (8 sc) Place marker to indicate beginning of rnd.

Note: Loop a short piece of yarn around any stitch to mark Rnd 1 as right side. Move stitch marker up with each rnd.

Rnd 2: 2 sc in each st around. (16 sc)

Rnd 3: (Sc in next st, 2 sc in next st) around. (24 sc)

Rnd 4: (Sc in next 2 sts, 2 sc in next st) around. (32 sc)

Rnd 5: (Sc in next 3 sts, 2 sc in next st) around. (40 sc)

Rnds 6–18: Sc in each st around.

Rnd 19: (Sc in next 3 sts, sk next st) around. (30 sc)

Rnd 20: (Sc in next 2 sts, sk next st) around. (20 sc)

Stuff body firmly.

Rnd 21: (Sc in next st, sk next st) around. (10 sc)

Rnd 22: (Sc in next st, sk next st) around. (5 sc)

Fasten off, leaving a long tail for sewing.

Use yarn needle and sew Rnd 22 closed.

Head

Rnd 1 (RS): With **B** and smaller hook, create magic ring, 6 sc in ring; do not join. (6 sc) Place stitch marker to indicate beginning of rnd.

Note: Loop a short piece of yarn around any stitch to mark Rnd 1 as right side. Move stitch marker up with each rnd.

Rnd 2: 2 sc in each st around. (12 sc)

Rnd 3: (Sc in next st, 2 sc in next st) around. (18 sc)

Rnd 4: (Sc in next 2 sts, 2 sc in next st) around. (24 sc)

Rnds 5–6: Sc in each st around.

Rnd 7: (Sc in next 3 sts, 2 sc in next st) around. (30 sc)

Rnds 8–9: Sc in each st around.

Rnd 10: (Sc in next 4 sts, 2 sc in next st) around. (36 sc)

Rnds 11–13: Sc in each st around.

Add safety eyes between Rnds 9 and 10 about 11 sts apart.

Rnd 14: (Sc in next 4 sts, sc2tog) around. (30 sc)

Fasten off.

Rnd 15: Join **A** in any st with larger hook, ch 1, sc in each st around; do not join.

Rnd 16: (Sc in next 4 sts, sk 1 st) around. (24 sc)

Rnd 17: Sc in each st around.

Rnd 18: (Sc in next 3 sts, sk 1 st) around. (18 sc)

Rnd 19: (Sc in next 2 sts, sk 1 st) around. (12 sc)

Stuff Head firmly.

Rnd 20: (Sc in next st, sk 1 st) around. (6 sc)

Fasten off, leaving a long tail for sewing.

Use yarn needle and close Rnd 20.

Neck

With **A** and larger hook, ch 18; join with sl st to first ch. (18 chs) Place stitch marker to indicate beginning of rnd.

Rnd 1 (RS): Ch 1, 18 sc in ring; do not join.

Note: Loop a short piece of yarn around any stitch to mark Rnd 1 as right side. Move stitch marker up with each rnd.

Rnds 2–3: Sc in each st around.

Rnd 4: (Sc in next 8 sts, sk 1 st). (16 sc)

Rnds 5–6: Sc in each st around.

Fasten off, leaving a long tail for sewing.

Ear (make 2)

Rnd 1 (RS): With **C** and smaller hook, create magic ring, 4 sc in ring; do not join. (4 sc) Place stitch marker to indicate beginning of rnd.

Note: Loop a short piece of yarn around any stitch to mark Rnd 1 as right side. Move stitch marker up with each rnd.

Rnd 2: 2 sc in each st around. (8 sc)

Rnd 3: (Sc in next st, 2 sc in next st) around. (12 sc)

Rnds 4–5: Sc in each st around.

Rnd 6: (Sc in next 2 sts, 2 sc in next st) around. (16 sc)

Rnds 7–8: Sc in each st around.

Rnd 9: (Sc in next 2 sts, sc2tog) around. (12 sc)

Rnd 10: Sc in each st around.

Fasten off, leaving a long tail for sewing.

Foot (make 4)

Rnd 1 (RS): With **C** and smaller hook, create magic ring, 10 sc in ring; do not join. (10 sc) Place stitch marker to indicate beginning of rnd.

Note: Loop a short piece of yarn around any stitch to mark Rnd 1 as right side. Move stitch marker up with each rnd.

Rnd 2: (Sc in next st, 2 sc in next st) around. (15 sc)

Rnd 3: Working in the BLO, sc in each st around.

Rnds 4–6: Sc in each st around.

Fasten off.

Rnd 7: Join **A** with larger hook in any st, ch 1, sc in first st, (ch 1, sk 1 st, sc in next st) around. (8 sc)

Rnd 8: Sc in each st around. (8 sc)

Fasten off, leaving a long tail for sewing.

Blanket

With **D** and smaller hook, ch 31.

Row 1 (RS): Sc in 2nd ch and in each ch across, turn. (30 sc)

Row 2: Ch 1, sc in each st across, turn.

Fasten off **D**, join **B**.

Rows 3–4: Ch 3 (counts as dc), dc in each st across, turn.
Fasten off **B**, join **D**.
Rows 5–6: Ch 1, sc in each st across, turn.
Fasten off.

Border

Rnd 1 (RS): With **E**, ch 1, 3 sc in first st, sc in next 28 sts, 3 sc in last st, sc evenly down ends of rows, 3 sc in first st of Row 1, sc in next 28 sts, 3 sc in last st, sc evenly down ends of rows; join with sl st to first sc.
Fasten off.

Fringe

For each corner fringe cut 3 strands of **E** 4 in (10 cm) long. Hold strands together and fold in half. Draw fold through corner of Blanket, forming a loop. Pull ends of fringe through this loop. Pull to tighten. Trim fringe evenly.

Assembly

Use photos as a guide.
Sew Feet on Body.
Sew Neck on Body.
Sew Head on Neck.
Stitch Ears to Head.
Stitch nose on Head with **C**.
Stitch Blanket on Body.

Walter the Bear

Besides being cuddly and cute, this supersize bear is fun to crochet! He is crocheted in only two colors, so it's a great beginner project.

Yarn

Knit Picks (WeCrochet) Tuff Puff; super bulky
    weight #6; 100% wool; 3.50 oz (100 g)/
    44 yd (40 m) per skein
- 8 skeins: 28063 Snickerdoodle (**A**)
- 1 skein each: 27213 Flamingo (**B**), 26851 Bark (**C**)
    (nose detail only)

Hook and Other Materials

- US size J-10 (6 mm) crochet hook
- Yarn needle
- Poly-fil stuffing
- Two 15 mm safety eyes
- Stitch markers
- 3 yards of ribbon (optional)

Finished Measurement

About 14 in (35.5 cm) tall

Gauge

11 sc and 11 rows/rounds = 4 in (10 cm)

Special Stitch

Invisible single crochet 2 together (sc2tog): Insert
    hook in the FLO of next 2 sts, yarn over and draw
    through both sts, yarn over and draw through 2
    loops on hook (1 stitch decreased).

Pattern Note

Bear is made in 10 pieces: Body, Head, 2 Arms, 2
    Legs, Nose, Ears, and Tail.

INSTRUCTIONS

Body

Rnd 1 (RS): With **A**, create magic ring, 8 sc in ring; do not join. (8 sc) Place marker to indicate beginning of rnd.

Note: Loop a short piece of yarn around any stitch to mark Rnd 1 as right side. Move stitch marker up with each rnd.

Rnd 2: 2 sc in each st around. (16 sc)

Rnd 3: (Sc in next st, 2 sc in next st) around. (24 sc)

Rnd 4: (Sc in next 2 sts, 2 sc in next st) around. (32 sc)

Rnd 5: (Sc in next 3 sts, 2 sc in next st) around. (40 sc)

Rnd 6: (Sc in next 4 sts, 2 sc in next st) around. (48 sc)

Rnd 7: (Sc in next 5 sts, 2 sc in next st) around. (56 sc)

Rnd 8: (Sc in next 6 sts, 2 sc in next st) around. (64 sc)

Rnds 9–21: Sc in each st around.

Rnd 22: (Sc in next 6 sts, sc2tog) around. (56 sc)

Rnd 23: Sc in each st around.

Rnd 24: (Sc in next 5 sts, sc2tog) around. (48 sc)

Rnd 25: Sc in each st around.

Rnd 26: (Sc in next 4 sts, sc2tog) around. (40 sc)

Rnd 27: (Sc in next 3 sts, sc2tog) around. (32 sc)

Rnd 28: (Sc in next 2 sts, sc2tog) around. (24 sc)

Stuff Body firmly.

Head

Rnd 29: 2 sc in each st around. (48 sc)

Rnd 30: (Sc in next 5 sts, 2 sc in next st) around. (56 sc)

Rnds 31–42: Sc in each st around.

Rnd 43: (Sc in next 5 sts, sc2tog) around. (48 sc)

Rnd 44: Sc in each st around.

Rnd 45: (Sc in next 4 sts, sc2tog) around. (40 sc)

Rnd 46: (Sc in next 3 sts, sc2tog) around. (32 sc)

Rnd 47: (Sc in next 2 sts, sc2tog) around. (24 sc)

Rnd 48: (Sc in next st, sc2tog) around. (16 sc)

Stuff head firmly.

Rnd 49: (Sc2tog) 8 times. (8 sc)

Fasten off, leaving a long tail for sewing.

Use yarn needle and close Rnd 49.

Arm (make 2)

Rnd 1 (RS): With **B**, create magic ring, 6 sc in ring; do not join. (6 sc) Place marker to indicate beginning of rnd.

Note: Loop a short piece of yarn around any stitch to mark Rnd 1 as right side. Move stitch marker up with each rnd.

Rnd 2: 2 sc in each st around. (12 sc)

Rnd 3: (Sc in next st, 2 sc in next st) around; join with sl st to first sc. (18 sc)

Fasten off.

Rnd 4: Join **A** in any st, ch 1, sc in each st around; join with sl st to first sc.

Rnd 5: Ch 1, sc in each st around; do not join.

Rnds 6–11: Sc in each st around.

Rnd 12: (Sc in next 7 sts, sc2tog) around. (16 sc)

Rnds 13–17: Sc in each st around.

Fasten off, leaving a long tail for sewing.

Stuff ends of Arms firmly, leaving top half unstuffed.

Leg (make 2)

Rnd 1 (RS): With **B**, create magic ring, 6 sc in ring; do not join. (6 sc) Place marker to indicate beginning of rnd.

Note: Loop a short piece of yarn around any stitch to mark Rnd 1 as right side. Move stitch marker up with each rnd.

Rnd 2: 2 sc in each st around. (12 sc)

Rnd 3: (Sc in next st, 2 sc in next st) around; join with sl st to first sc. (18 sc)

Fasten off.

Rnd 4: Join A in any st, ch 1, sc in each st around; join with sl st to first sc.

Rnds 5–6: Sc in each st around.

Rnd 7: (Sc2tog) 9 times.

Fasten off, leaving a long tail for sewing.

Ear (make 2)

Rnd 1 (RS): With **A**, create magic ring, 5 sc in ring; do not join. (5 sc) Place marker to indicate beginning of rnd.

Note: Loop a short piece of yarn around any stitch to mark Rnd 1 as right side. Move stitch marker up with each rnd.

Rnd 2: 2 sc in each rnd. (10 sc)

Rnd 3: (2 sc in next st, sc in next 4 sts) around. (12 sc)

Rnd 4: (Sc in next 2 sts, sc2tog) around. (9 sc)

Fasten off, leaving a long tail for sewing.

Do not stuff.

Nose

Rnd 1 (RS): With **A**, create magic ring, 5 sc in ring; do not join. (5 sc) Place marker to indicate beginning of rnd.

Note: Loop a short piece of yarn around any stitch to mark Rnd 1 as right side. Move stitch marker up with each rnd.

Rnd 2: 2 sc in each rnd. (10 sc)
Rnd 3: (Sc in next 4 sts, 2 sc in next st) around. (12 sc)
Rnds 4–5: Sc in each st around.
Fasten off, leaving a long tail for sewing.

Tail

Rnd 1 (RS): With **A**, create magic ring, 5 sc in ring; do not join. (5 sc) Place marker to indicate beginning of rnd.
Note: Loop a short piece of yarn around any stitch to mark Rnd 1 as right side. Move stitch marker up with each rnd.
Rnd 2: 2 sc in each rnd. (10 sc)
Rnds 3–4: Sc in each st around.
Fasten off, leaving a long tail for sewing.

Assembly

Use photos as a guide.
Sew Ears and Nose on Head.
Use **C** and stitch on Nose detail.
Sew Arms on each side of Body.
Sew Legs on Body, stuffing before closing.
Sew Tail on back of Body, stuffing before closing.
Tie Ribbon around neck and knot to secure.

Sweetheart Hippo

This beginner-friendly animal is such a sweetheart! I had to make it in my favorite color, purple, but you can make it in any color for your child. Enjoy mixing and matching your favorite colors to create this adorable hippo.

Yarn

Cascade Yarns Cherub Bulky; super bulky weight #6; 55% nylon/45% acrylic; 7.05 oz (200 g)/ 131 yd (120 m) per skein

- 4 skeins: 87 Dahlia

Hook and Other Materials

- US size J-10 (6 mm) crochet hook
- Yarn needle
- Poly-fil stuffing
- Two 15 mm safety eyes
- Stitch markers

Finished Measurement

About 17.5 in (44.5 cm) tall

Gauge

11 sc and 11 rows/rounds = 4 in (10 cm)

Special Stitch

Invisible single crochet 2 together (sc2tog): Insert hook in the FLO of next 2 sts, yarn over and draw through both sts, yarn over and draw through 2 loops on hook (1 stitch decreased).

Pattern Note

Hippo is made in 10 pieces: Body, Head, 2 Arms, 2 Legs, Nose, 2 Ears, and Tail.

INSTRUCTIONS

Body

Rnd 1 (RS): Create magic ring, 8 sc in ring; do not join. (8 sc) Place marker to indicate beginning of rnd.

Note: Loop a short piece of yarn around any stitch to mark Rnd 1 as right side. Move stitch marker up with each rnd.

Rnd 2: 2 sc in each st around. (16 sc)

Rnd 3: (Sc in next st, 2 sc in next st) around. (24 sc)

Rnd 4: (Sc in next 2 sts, 2 sc in next st) around. (32 sc)

Rnd 5: (Sc in next 3 sts, 2 sc in next st) around. (40 sc)

Rnd 6: (Sc in next 4 sts, 2 sc in next st) around. (48 sc)

Rnd 7: (Sc in next 5 sts, 2 sc in next st) around. (56 sc)

Rnd 8: (Sc in next 6 sts, 2 sc in next st) around. (64 sc)

Rnd 9: Sc in each st around.

Rnd 10: (Sc in next 7 sts, 2 sc in next st) around. (72 sc)

Rnds 11–30: Sc in each st around.

Rnd 31: Sc in next 18 sts, (sc2tog, sc in next 4 sts) 2 times, sc2tog, sc in next 8 sts, sc2tog, (sc in next 4 sts, sc2tog) 2 times, sc in next 18 sts. (66 sc)

Rnd 32: Sc in next 18 sts, (sc2tog, sc in next 3 sts) 2 times, sc2tog, sc in next 6 sts, sc2tog, (sc in next 3 sts, sc2tog) 2 times, sc in next 18 sts. (60 sc)

Rnd 33: Sc in next 18 sts, (sc2tog, sc in next 2 sts) 2 times, sc2tog, sc in next 4 sts, sc2tog, (sc in next 2 sts, sc2tog) 2 times, sc in next 18 sts. (54 sc)

Rnd 34: Sc in next 18 sts, (sc2tog, sc in next st) 2 times, sc2tog, sc in next 2 sts, sc2tog, (sc in next st, sc2tog) 2 times, sc in next 18 sts. (48 sc)

Rnds 35–36: Sc in each st around.

Rnd 37: (Sc in next 6 sts, sc2tog) around. (42 sc)
Rnd 38: Sc in each st around.
Rnd 39: (Sc in next 5 sts, sc2tog) around. (36 sc)
Rnd 40: Sc in each st around.
Rnd 41: (Sc in next 4 sts, sc2tog) around. (30 sc)
Rnd 42: (Sc in next 3 sts, sc2tog) around. (24 sc)
Stuff Body firmly.

Head

Rnd 43: 2 sc in each st around. (48 sc)
Rnd 44: (Sc in next 5 sts, 2 sc in next st) around. (56 sc)
Rnd 45: (Sc in next 6 sts, 2 sc in next st) around. (64 sc)
Rnd 46: (Sc in next 7 sts, 2 sc in next st) around. (72 sc)
Rnds 47–53: Sc in each st around.
Rnd 54: (Sc in next 7 sts, sc2tog) around. (64 sc)
Rnd 55: Sc in each st around.

Rnd 56: (Sc in next 6 sts, sc2tog) around. (56 sc)
Rnd 57: Sc in each st around.
Rnd 58: (Sc in next 5 sts, sc2tog) around. (48 sc)
Rnds 59–63: Sc in each st around.
Rnd 64: (Sc in next 4 sts, sc2tog) around. (40 sc)
Rnd 65: (Sc in next 3 sts, sc2tog) around. (32 sc)
Rnd 66: (Sc in next 2 sts, sc2tog) around. (24 sc)
Rnd 67: (Sc in next st, sc2tog) around. (16 sc)
Rnd 68: (Sc2tog) 8 times. (8 sc)
Fasten off, leaving a long tail for sewing.
Use yarn needle to close Rnd 68.

Arm (make 2)

Rnd 1 (RS): Create magic ring, 6 sc in ring; do not join. (6 sc) Place marker to indicate beginning of rnd.
Note: Loop a short piece of yarn around any stitch to mark Rnd 1 as right side. Move stitch marker up with each rnd.

Rnd 2: 2 sc in each st around. (12 sc)

Rnd 3: (Sc in next st, 2 sc in next st) around. (18 sc)

Rnd 4: (Sc in next 2 sts, 2 sc in next st) around. (24 sc)

Rnd 5: Working in the BLO, sc in each st around.

Rnds 6–10: Sc in each st around.

Rnd 11: (Sc in next 2 sts, sc2tog) around. (18 sc)

Rnds 12–24: Sc in each st around.

Fasten off, leaving a long tail for sewing.

Stuff ends of Arms firmly, leaving top half unstuffed.

Leg (make 2)

Rnd 1 (RS): Create magic ring, 6 sc in ring; do not join. (6 sc) Place marker to indicate beginning of rnd.

Note: Loop a short piece of yarn around any stitch to mark Rnd 1 as right side. Move stitch marker up with each rnd.

Rnd 2: 2 sc in each st around. (12 sc)

Rnd 3: (Sc in next st, 2 sc in next st) around. (18 sc)

Rnd 4: (Sc in next 2 sts, 2 sc in next st) around. (24 sc)

Rnd 5: (Sc in next 3 sts, 2 sc in next st) around. (30 sc)

Rnd 6: Working in the BLO, sc in each st around.

Rnds 7–10: Sc in each st around.

Rnd 11: (Sc in next 3 sts, sc2tog) around. (24 sc)

Rnds 12–28: Sc in each st around.

Fasten off, leaving a long tail for sewing.

Stuff ends of Legs firmly, leaving top half unstuffed.

Nose

Ch 11.

Rnd 1 (RS): Sc in 2nd ch from hook, sc in next 8 chs, 3 sc in last ch; working on opposite side of ch, sc in next 8 chs, 2 sc in last ch; join with sl st to first sc. (22 sc)

Rnd 2: Ch 1, 2 sc in first sc, sc in next 8 sts, 2 sc in next sc, sc in next st, 2 sc in next st, sc in next 8 sts, 2 sc in next st, sc in last st; join with sl st to first sc. (26 sc)

Rnd 3: Ch 1, sc in first st, 2 sc in next st, sc in next 8 sts, 2 sc in next st, sc in next 2 sts, 2 sc in next st, sc in next 9 sts, 2 sc in next st, sc in last st; join with sl st to first sc. (30 sc)

Rnd 4: Ch 1, sc in first st, sc in next st, 2 sc in next st, sc in next 10 sts, 2 sc in next st, sc in next 3 sts, 2 sc in next st, sc in next 10 sts, 2 sc in next st, sc in last st; join with sl st to first sc. (34 sc)

Rnds 5–6: Ch 1, sc in each st around; join with sl st to first sc.

Fasten off, leaving a long tail for sewing.

Ear (make 2)

Ch 4.

Rnd 1: Sl st in 2nd ch from hook, sc in next ch, 5 dc in last ch, working on opposite side of ch, sc in next ch, sl st in next ch; join with sl st to first sl st.

Fasten off, leaving a long tail for sewing.

Tail

Ch 9.

Row 1 (RS): Sc in 2nd ch from hook and in each ch across, turn. (7 sc)

Rows 2–3: Ch 1, sc in each st across, turn.

Fasten off, leaving a long tail for sewing.

Sew Row 1 to 3 lengthwise.

Cut 4 strands 4 in (10 cm) long. Hold strands together and fold in half. Draw fold through one end of Tail, forming a loop. Pull ends of fringe through this loop. Pull to tighten. Trim evenly.

Assembly

Use photos as a guide.

Sew Arms and Legs on Body.

Sew Nose on Head, stuffing before closing.

Sew Ears on Head.

Sew Tail on back of Body.

Smiley the Sloth

Enjoy making this slow-motion creature in a super-fast way with jumbo #7 yarn! The sloth is the largest animal in the book, and you will find yourself carrying it on your hip just like a toddler. It's the most snuggly and friendly animal in the collection—you definitely need to make one!

Yarn

Lion Brand Yarns Go For Faux Thick & Quick; jumbo weight #7; 100% polyester; 4.2 oz (120 g)/ 24 yd (22 m) per skein
- 13 skeins: 323-209 Chow Chow (**A**)

Lion Brand Yarns Wool-Ease Thick & Quick; super bulky weight #6; 80% acrylic/20% wool; 6 oz (170 g)/106 yd (97 m) per skein
- 1 skein each: 640-99 Fisherman (**B**), 640-153 Black (**C**)

Hooks and Other Materials

- US size J-10 (6 mm) crochet hook
- US size N-13 (9 mm) crochet hook
- Yarn needle
- Poly-fil stuffing
- Two 15 mm safety eyes
- Stitch markers

Finished Measurement

About 17 in (43 cm) tall

Gauge

With **B** and smaller hook, 11 sc and 11 rows/rounds = 4 in (10 cm)

Special Stitch

Invisible single crochet 2 together (sc2tog): Insert hook in the FLO of next 2 sts, yarn over and draw through both sts, yarn over and draw through 2 loops on hook (1 stitch decreased).

Pattern Notes

- Sloth is made in 21 pieces: Body, Head, 2 Eye Patches, Face, 2 Legs, 2 Arms, and 12 Fingers.
- This amigurumi is primarily made with a jumbo #7 yarn, but crocheting a mini with medium-weight #4 yarn will not convert to similar proportions.

INSTRUCTIONS

Body

Rnd 1 (RS): With **A** and larger hook, create magic ring, 10 sc in ring; do not join. (10 sc) Place marker to indicate beginning of rnd.

Note: Loop a short piece of yarn around any stitch to mark Rnd 1 as right side. Move stitch marker up with each rnd.

Rnd 2: 2 sc in each st around. (20 sc)

Rnd 3: (Sc in next st, 2 sc in next st) around. (30 sc)

Rnd 4: (Sc in next 2 sts, 2 sc in next st) around. (40 sc)

Rnd 5: (Sc in next 7 sts, 2 sc in next st) around. (45 sc)

Rnds 6–17: Sc in each st around.

Rnd 18: (Sc in next 8 sts, sk 1 st) around. (40 sc)

Rnd 19: (Sc in next 3 sts, sk 1 st) around. (30 sc)

Rnd 20: Sc in each st around.

Rnd 21: (Sc in next 2 sts, sk 1 st) around. (20 sc)

Rnd 22: Sc in each st around.

Rnd 23: (Sc in next 3 sts, sk 1 st) around. (15 sc)

Head

Rnd 24: 2 sc in each st around. (30 sc)

Rnd 25: (Sc in next 2 sts, 2 sc in next st) around. (40 sc)

Rnd 26: (Sc in next 7 sts, 2 sc in next st) around. (45 sc)

Rnds 27–34: Sc in each st around.

Rnd 35: (Sc in next 8 sts, sk 1 st) around. (40 sc)

Rnd 36: (Sc in next 3 sts, sk 1 st) around. (30 sc)

Rnd 37: (Sc in next 2 sts, sk 1 st) around. (20 sc)

Rnd 38: (Sc in next st, sk 1 st) around. (10 sc)

Rnd 39: (Sc in next st, sk 1 st) around. (5 sc)

Fasten off, leaving a long tail for sewing.

Use yarn needle and close Rnd 39.

Arm (make 2)

With **A** and larger hook, ch 12; join with sl st to first ch.

Rnd 1: Ch 1, 12 sc in ring; do not join. (12 sc)

Rnds 2–14: Sc in each st around.

Fasten off **A**, join **B**.

Rnds 15–16: With smaller hook, sc in each st around. (12 sc)

Stuff Arm lightly.

Finger 1

Rnd 17: Sc in next 4 sts, sk 8 sts (mark 1st skipped st); do not join.

Rnds 18–20: Sc in next 4 sts; join with sl st to first sc.

Fasten off, leaving a long tail for sewing.

Use yarn needle to close Rnd 20.

Do not stuff Finger.

Finger 2
Rnd 1: Join in marked st, ch 1, sc in next 2 sts, sk 4 sts (mark 1st skipped st), sc in next 2 sts; do not join.
Rnds 2–4: Sc in each st around; join with sl st to first sc.
Fasten off, leaving a long tail for sewing.
Use yarn needle to close Rnd 4.

Do not stuff Finger.
Stuff Hand firmly before completing last Finger.

Finger 3
Rnd 1: Join in marked st, ch 1, sc in next 4 sts; do not join.
Rnds 2–4: Sc in each st around; join with sl st to first sc.
Fasten off, leaving a long tail for sewing.
Use yarn needle to close Rnd 4.
Do not stuff Finger.

Leg (make 2)
With **A** and larger hook, ch 13; join with sl st to first ch.
Rnd 1: Ch 1, 13 sc in ring; do not join. (13 sc)
Rnds 2–13: Sc in each st around.
Rnd 14: Sc2tog, sc in next 11 sts. (12 sc)
Fasten off **A**, join **B**.
Rnds 15–16: With smaller hook, sc in each st around. (12 sc)
Stuff Leg lightly.
Complete Fingers 1–3 as for Arm.

Eye Patch (make 1 of each)
Left
With **C** and smaller hook, ch 7.

Rnd 1: Sl st in 2nd ch from hook, sc in next ch, hdc in next ch, dc in next 2 chs, 6 dc in last ch; working on opposite side of ch, hdc in next ch, sc in next ch, sl st in last 2 chs; join with sl st to first sl st.

Fasten off, leaving a long tail for sewing.

Add safety eye.

Right
With **C** and smaller hook, ch 7.

Rnd 1: Sl st in 2nd ch from hook, sl st in next ch, sc in next ch, hdc in next ch, 6 dc in last ch; working on opposite side of ch, dc in next 2 chs, hdc in next ch, sc in next ch, sl st in last ch; join with sl st in first sl st.

Fasten off, leaving a long tail for sewing.

Add safety eye.

Face Assembly
Sew Eye Patches on Face.

Use yarn needle and wrap **A** around the edge of Face.

With **C**, stitch on nose and mouth.

Face
With **B** and smaller hook, ch 11.

Row 1: 2 sc in 2nd ch from hook, sc in next 8 chs, 2 sc in next ch, turn. (12 sc)

Row 2: Ch 1, 2 sc in first st, sc in next 10 sts, 2 sc in next st, turn. (14 sc)

Row 3: Sc in each st across, turn.

Row 4: Ch 1, 2 sc in first st, sc in next 12 sts, 2 sc in next st, turn. (16 sc)

Row 5: Sc in each st across, turn.

Row 6: Ch 1, 2 sc in first st, sc in next 14 sts, 2 sc in next st, turn. (18 sc)

Rows 7–9: Ch 1, sc in st across, turn.

Row 10: Ch 1, sc2tog, sc in next 14 sts, sc2tog, turn. (16 sc)

Row 11: Ch 1, sc in each st across, turn.

Row 12: Ch 1, sc2tog, sc in next 12 sts, sc2tog, turn. (14 sc)

Row 13: Ch 1, sc2tog, sc in next 10 sts, sc2tog, turn. (12 sc)

Row 14: Ch 1, sc2tog, sc in next 8 sts, sc2tog, turn. (10 sc)

Fasten off.

Assembly
Use photos as a guide.

Sew Arms and Legs on Body.

Sew Face on Head.

HOW TO READ THE PATTERNS

SYMBOLS AND TERMS

* : Work instructions following * as many more times as indicated in addition to the first time.

( ): Work enclosed instructions as many times as specified by the number immediately following or work all enclosed instructions in the stitch or space indicated or contains explanatory remarks.

( ) **at end of row or rnd:** The number of stitches or spaces you should have after completing that row or round.

GAUGE

Exact gauge is essential for proper size. Before beginning your project, make a sample swatch in the yarn and hook specified. After completing the swatch, measure it, counting your stitches and rows carefully. If your swatch is larger or smaller than specified, make another, changing hook size to get the correct gauge. Keep trying until you find the size hook that will give you the specified gauge.

SKILL LEVELS

Note: All projects in this book are either Easy or Intermediate level.

Beginner: Projects for first-time crocheters using basic stitches. Minimal shaping.

Easy: Projects using yarn with basic stitches, repetitive stitch patterns, simple color changes, and simple shaping and finishing.

Intermediate: Projects using a variety of techniques, such as basic lace patterns or color patterns, and mid-level shaping and finishing.

Experienced: Projects with intricate stitch patterns, techniques, and dimensions, such as nonrepeating patterns, multicolor techniques, fine threads, small hooks, detailed shaping, and refined finishing.

YARN

You will find listed for each pattern the specific yarn(s) and colors I used to crochet the pattern, plus how many skeins you'll need. Also included is that specific yarn's yarn weight. You'll find this information on the label of every skein of yarn you buy, and it ranges from #0 lace weight to #7 jumbo weight. If you can't find the specific yarn I used or you'd like to use something else, knowing the yarn weight will help you pick another yarn that will have the same gauge.

Standard Yarn Weight System

Categories of yarn, gauge ranges, and recommended needle and hook sizes

Yarn Weight Symbol & Category Names	0 LACE	1 SUPER FINE	2 FINE	3 LIGHT	4 MEDIUM	5 BULKY	6 SUPER BULKY	7 JUMBO
Type of Yarns in Category	Fingering, 10-Count Crochet Thread	Sock, Fingering, Baby	Sport, Baby	DK, Light Worsted	Worsted, Afghan, Aran	Chunky, Craft, Rug	Bulky, Roving	Jumbo, Roving
Knit Gauge Range in Stockinette Stitch to 4 inches*	33–40 sts**	27–32 sts	23–26 sts	21–24 st	16–20 sts	12–15 sts	7–11 sts	6 sts and fewer
Recommended Needle in Metric Size Range	1.5–2.25 mm	2.25–3.25 mm	3.25–3.75 mm	3.75–4.5 mm	4.5–5.5 mm	5.5–8 mm	8–12.75 mm	12.75 mm and larger
Recommended Needle in U.S. Size Range	000 to 1	1 to 3	3 to 5	5 to 7	7 to 9	9 to 11	11 to 17	17 and larger
Crochet Gauge Ranges in Single Crochet to 4 inches*	32–42 double crochets**	21–32 sts	16–20 sts	12–17 sts	11–14 sts	8–11 sts	7–9 sts	6 sts and fewer
Recommended Hook in Metric Size Range	Steel*** 1.6–1.4 mm Regular hook 2.25 mm	2.25–3.5 mm	3.5–4.5 mm	4.5–5.5 mm	5.5–6.5 mm	6.5–9 mm	9–15 mm	15 mm and larger
Recommended Hook in U.S. Size Range	Steel 6, 7, 8*** Regular hook B–1	B–1 to E–4	E–4 to 7	7 to I–9	I–9 to K–10½	K–10½ to M–13	M–13 to Q	Q and larger

* GUIDELINES ONLY: The above reflect the most commonly used gauges and needle or hook sizes for specific yarn categories.
** Lace weight yarns are usually knitted or crocheted on larger needles and hooks to create lacy, openwork patterns. Accordingly, a gauge range is difficult to determine. Always follow the gauge stated in your pattern.
*** Steel crochet hooks are sized differently from regular hooks—the higher the number, the smaller the hook, which is the reverse of regular hook sizing.

*Source: Craft Yarn Council of America's **www.YarnStandards.com***

HOOKS AND OTHER MATERIALS

Items you will need to complete the patterns in this book include crochet hooks, stitch markers, pins, scissors, yarn, a ruler, a yarn needle, and other items as given in the list for each pattern.

- **Crochet hooks:** Each pattern will list the crochet hook needed for that project. Always start with the hook size stated and check the gauge before starting the project. Change the hook size as necessary to obtain the correct gauge so that the project will be finished in the correct size.
- **Stitch markers:** Stitch markers are used to mark specific stitches in a pattern. If you do not have access to ready-made markers, use a piece of scrap yarn or even a bobby pin to mark the stitch.
- **Yarn needle:** The yarn needle is a large needle with a big eye suitable for yarn, used to sew different pieces together and for weaving in ends.

NOTES ON THE INSTRUCTIONS

- When a number appears before the stitch name, such as 3 dc, work these stitches into the same stitch, for example, "3 dc into the next stitch."
- When only one stitch is to be worked into each of a number of stitches, it can be written like this, for example, "1 sc in each of next 3 sts." When a number appears after a chain, for example, ch 10, this means work the number of chains indicated.
- The asterisks mark a specific set of instructions that are repeated; for example, "* 2 sc in next st, 1 dc in next st, rep from * across" means repeat the stitches from the asterisk to the next given instruction.
- When instructions are given with parentheses, it can mean three things. For example, "(2 dc, ch 1, 2 dc) in the next st" means work 2 dc, ch 1, 2 dc all into the same stitch. It can also mean a set of stitches repeated a number of times, for example, "(sc in next st, 2 sc in next st) 6 times." Last, the number(s) given at the end of a row or round in parentheses denote(s) the number of stitches or spaces you should have on that row or round.
- Be sure to read the Special Stitch(es) and Pattern Note(s) sections before beginning a project. You'll find any new stitches and helpful hints there, and reading these notes will often clear up any questions about the project.

ABBREVIATIONS

beg	begin/begins/beginning		**rep(s)**	repeat(s)
BLO	back loop only		**rnd(s)**	round(s)
ch(s)	chain/chains		**RS**	right side
ch-	refers to chain or space previously made		**sc**	single crochet
ch sp(s)	chain space(s)		**sc2tog**	single crochet 2 stitches together
cm	centimeter(s)		**sk**	skip
dc	double crochet		**sl st(s)**	slip stitch(es)
FLO	front loop only		**sp(s)**	space(s)
g	gram(s)		**st(s)**	stitch(es)
hdc	half double crochet		**tog**	together
in	inch(es)		**WS**	wrong side
mm	millimeter(s)		**yd(s)**	yard(s)
oz	ounce(s)			

STITCH GUIDE

How to Hold Your Hook

There are different ways that you can hold your hook, but I want to show you two of the most common. Try both and use the one that feels most comfortable.

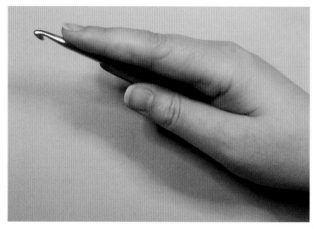

Knife Hold: Hold the hook in your hand like you would a knife. Your hand is over the hook, using your thumb and middle finger to control the hook while the pointer finger is on top guiding the yarn.

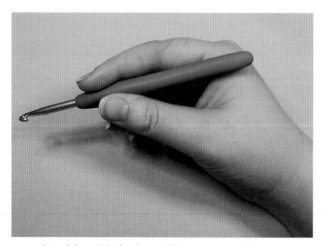

Pencil Hold: Hold the hook like you would a pencil. The hook is cradled in your hand resting on your middle finger.

Slipknot

This adjustable knot will begin every crochet project.

1. Make a loop in the yarn.

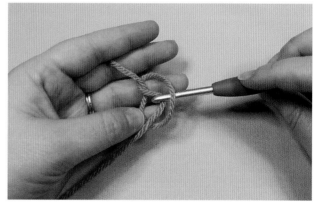

2. With crochet hook or finger, grab the yarn from the skein and pull through the loop.

3. Pull tight on the yarn and adjust to create the first loop.

Chain (ch)

The chain provides the foundation for your stitches at the beginning of a pattern. It can also serve as a stitch within a pattern and can be used to create an open effect.

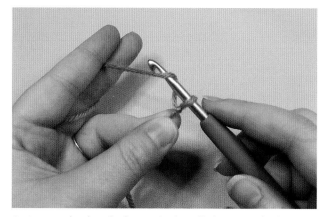

1. Insert the hook through the slipknot and place the yarn over the hook by passing the hook in front of the yarn.

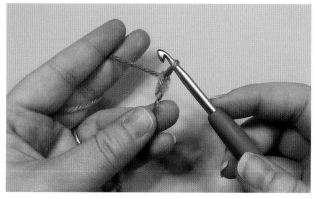

2. Keeping the yarn taut (but not too tight) pull the hook back through the loop with the yarn. Ch 1 is complete.

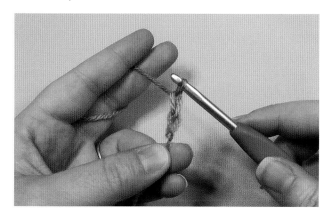

3. Repeat Steps 1 and 2 to create multiple chains.

Single Crochet (sc)

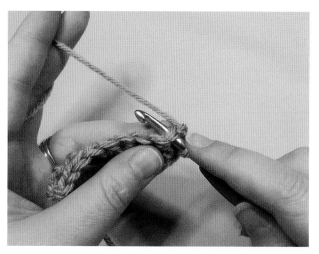

1. Insert the hook from the front of the stitch to the back and yarn over.

2. Pull the yarn back through the stitch: 2 loops on the hook.

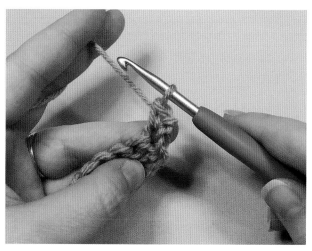

3. Yarn over and draw through both loops on the hook to complete.

129

Working into a Stitch

Unless specified otherwise, you will insert your hook under both loops to crochet any stitch.

Working into Back Loop or Front Loop

At times you will be instructed to work in the front loop only (FLO) or the back loop only (BLO) of a stitch to create a texture within the pattern.

Inserting hook to crochet into the front loop only (FLO) of a stitch.

Inserting hook to crochet into the back loop only (BLO) of a stitch.

Slip Stitch (sl st)

The slip stitch is used to join one stitch to another or to join a stitch to another point. It can also be used within the pattern as a stitch without height.

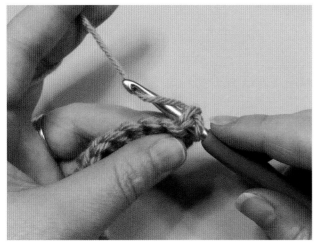

1. Insert the hook from the front of the stitch to the back of the stitch and yarn over.

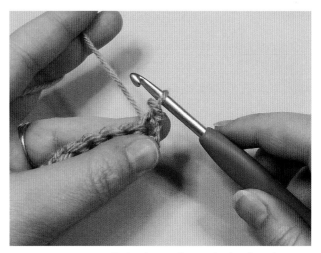

3. Continue to pull the loop through the first loop on the hook to finish.

2. Pull the yarn back through the stitch: 2 loops on the hook.

Half Double Crochet (hdc)

1. Yarn over from the back to the front over the hook.

3. Yarn over and pull the yarn back through the stitch: 3 loops on the hook.

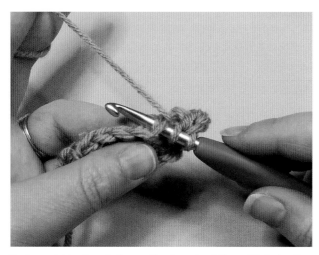

2. Insert the hook from the front of the stitch to the back.

4. Yarn over and draw through all 3 loops on the hook to complete.

Double Crochet (dc)

1. Yarn over and insert the hook from the front of the stitch to the back.

3. Yarn over and draw the yarn through the first 2 loops on the hook: 2 loops on the hook.

2. Yarn over and pull the yarn back through the stitch: 3 loops on the hook.

4. Yarn over and draw the yarn through the last 2 loops on the hook to complete.

Invisible Single Crochet 2 Together (sc2tog)

When working within a pattern, use the invisible single crochet 2 together when sc2tog is used to create a less visible decrease:

1. Insert the hook in the FLO of the next 2 stitches and yarn over.

2. Draw through both stitches, yarn over, and draw through 2 loops on the hook (counts as one sc).

Invisible Join

1. Complete your last stitch, cut the yarn leaving a long end, and pull the yarn all the way through the last stitch/loop.

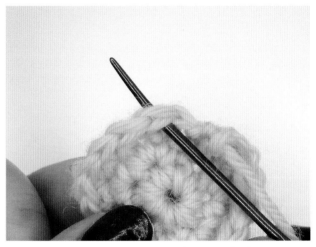

2. Thread the needle with the long end, skip 1 stitch, and insert the yarn needle from the front to the back of the next stitch.

Magic Ring

3. Skip the skipped stitch, and insert the yarn needle into the last stitch in the back loop from left to right (photo shows which back loop to use, but not in the direction; insert left to right).

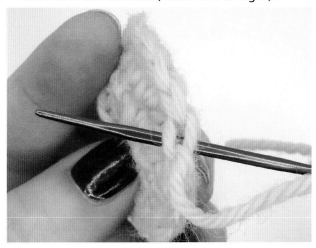

4. Pull the yarn loosely to create a new loop over the skipped loop. Photo shows how the invisible join creates a "loop" to finish the work. Weave in the ends on the wrong side of the work.

1. Hold the end of the yarn with pinky and ring finger, and wrap the yarn around the pointer finger as shown.

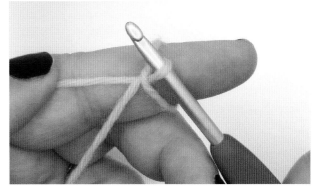

2. Insert the hook through the loop on pointer finger and pull up the loop.

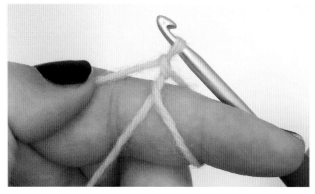

3. Chain one. This is an important step.

5. When you have completed the pattern directions, pull the beginning yarn tail until the center opening is tight and closed. Knot on the wrong side to hold in place securely.

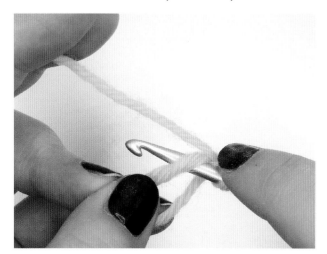

4. Follow the pattern and crochet into the loop and OVER the tail at the same time.

Color Change

When changing colors without fastening off, use this technique:

1. Complete your given stitch until the last pull through.

3. Continue working with the joined color.

2. Yarn over the next color and pull through to finish the stitch and color change. Cut or drop the yarn from the original color.

ACKNOWLEDGMENTS

I could not have completed this book without my husband, Jason. He keeps me laughing and encourages me to be creative in all my projects!

To my eagle-eye pattern editors, Christina Romich and Vicky Heimbecker: I appreciate your many hours of edits, tests, and patience. And I can't forget to thank my many testers . . . I love how this book has come together, and I am grateful for all those who have been a part of the process.

Photography for this book was by Heather with Heartstrings Photography in her beautiful studio in Huntsville, Alabama.